What makes a man a true man?

Published by Defassa
Publishing partner: Paragon Publishing, Rothersthorpe
First published 2014
© Defassa 2014-2025

williamdefassa@gmail.com
The rights of Defassa to be identified as the author of this work have been asserted
by him in accordance with the Copyright, Designs and Patents Act of 1988.

ISBN 978-1-78792-113-9

Book design, layout and production management by Into Print
www.intoprint.net
+44 (0)1604 832149

Third edition 2025

This Edition is Dedicated

To and For

GRACE

Love, DADDY

From the Author

A TRUE DEMOCRACY is a form of governing a nation in which all ethical, rational, equitable, and moral laws are upheld and enforced by that supreme authority granted to the common man by Nature and its creator to defend and act to ensure the well-being of all forms of life.

When the political, religious, commercial, or military interests of the state deny their subservient roles within a humane and civilised society, and begin to threated the well-being and freedoms of the common man, then it becomes his absolute duty to create and proclaim a Plebiscite – a decree that demands a reformation of that constitution of a nation that allows and encourages the state to become a democratic dictatorship.

Contents

Preface

IT IS ONLY universally valid cultures that can make a man's existence worthwhile and meaningful, just as it is only true men acting together that can create such a reality.

Thus, before all else it is the duty of every man to study, learn and understand those timeless and immortal truths that will give them those intellectual tools that are necessary for them to realise what being a true man actually is.

Once men understand their right and proper role within existence then and only then will they possess the moral and ethical authority to create universally valid cultures that alone have the ability to ensure that their members live enjoyable and stable lives and that the seeds of life are protected from all those that seek to control and destroy what they cannot possess themselves.

This book is written to be studied and not simply read. It is written to prove that no matter what others have said or done and no matter what they believe nothing can alter those eternal truths that are the cultural heritage of all men.

This book will enable the reader to become a new and powerful force that will not only be given the opportunity to become immortal but that will become a happy and useful entity that will be welcomed in this and any other existence.

Masculism

TRUTH IS WHAT is real and reality is dependent upon how things are presented to us. This book presents those truths necessary for those interested in knowing what being a *TRUE MAN* means.

Introduction

NO MATTER WHAT has, is or will be said; no matter how many times or by whom; no matter what political, religious, cultural or military regime we live under; no matter who or what we are, no creator, no god, no authority, no power now or ever can alter the truth.

Truth is what is real, and reality is dependent upon how things are presented to us.

This book presents you with the intellectual means to discover those necessary truths that are essential for you to fulfil your purpose upon this planet. Once you uncover for yourself your proper role within existence you have a choice – remain yourself or become a *TRUE MAN*.

1 The Parasitic Nature of Humans

As IT CAN be commonly observed that intelligence must be limited whilst stupidity isn't, then it is reasonable to conclude that the human world must be composed of different and differing types of being.

The first and most important type can be called true men, for they are nature's choice, and to these creatures has been granted the intellectual capacity that enables them to fulfil their natural functions of protecting the seeds of life and of creating viable and coherent cultures.

There are however many other types of being whose sole purpose in existence is to make this planet the most unjust, miserable and pointless place on which to exist.

The second group, though composed of differing types, can be classified as perverts, for they spare no effort nor expense in making this world as unfair and as perverted from the intentions of nature as possible.

Since the dawn of time, they have mounted a never-ending quest to entrap and enslave, in order that they may exist in some parasitic panacea, elevated into self-appointed positions of power.

To maintain such unnatural positions of perverted power, they are obliged to distort truth and reality.

They must hire thugs and henchmen, to ensure that the complete control they exercise over the assets and common wealth of those nations which they infest is never seriously challenged by the poor and dispossessed.

To avoid direct confrontation, they readily control how reality is presented to their submissive supporters, by only allowing their lapdogs a licence to broadcast their own version of reality. To compound and confuse simple issues, they possess a ludicrous array of exceedingly complex rules, regulations and laws to which honesty and straightforwardness are strangers.

To function as true parasites, they must distract an already distraught domesticated society by encouraging all forms of division, and by openly adopting divisive measures in order to prevent any cohesive social structures and movements arising to challenge their supremacy.

This world ordering of everybody about and the necessary attendant inquisitions to ensure that their commands are being obeyed have reached a pinnacle of perfection, being honed and polished by science, numeracy and electronics into an organised thuggery known as western democracies.

Man, nature's first truly rational creature has, since the beginning of time, been under attack.

Being the first animal given the power to reason as to how one object can be made relative to and be judged comparable with another, he thus became aware not only of himself but also that this relativity was governed by rules and regulations far older than his environment and belonged to a time before even the creation of the universe.

Thus, the first act of man was to form a culture that would enable him to embody those ideas that his intellect had chosen to represent what was right, proper and fair for himself, his family and his society into an objectified and easily accessible and useable form.

These ideals, refined and cultivated by time were designed by man to enable other men, who are responsible for protecting and creating the culture of their nations, to access those hopes, aspirations and dreams that form the basis of and the reason for life and to use those precepts to become true men.

No other creature and not all humans have been granted this degree of intellectual capacity that enables them to create stable non-exclusive cultures based upon that which is proper and fitting for each type of person to ensure a just and dignified existence.

Coherent, all-inclusive cultures engender their own safeguards which allow others to judge that which is unjust, perverse and wrong and thus permits them to discriminate against those who would distort truth and reality, justice and fairness for their own perverted ends. This gift of discernment has been entrusted to men in its most complete form and can only be passed from one generation to another through an extensive and comprehensive system of educating those able and willing to learn those timeless and universal ideas that separate the barbarian from the civilised and the injustice of animal greed from the generosity of equality.

There are many dangers to a successful transmission of ideas between peoples. The greatest of these is to restrict the cultural and intellectual freedom of true men to protect their ideals not only from unjustifiable contamination by the distorted dogmas of perverted sectarian bigots but from those perverted practices that are endemic to and in sick societies that always wish others to be brought down to a level as slavish and morally bankrupt as themselves.

If any man therefore accepts those challenges which are a necessary part of life and declares himself honour bound to protect his intellect and rationality, to protect the seeds of life, to fight to protect the innocent, no matter the cost, then he can consider himself a true man.

If true men should fail then though they themselves will reap those rewards that await all those who act in the name of justice equality and fairness with honour and dignity those left behind will turn into those wild irrational creatures that we see paraded before us as the new cultural ideal, the submissive slave, deodorised and sanitised, emasculated and integrated into that great one world theory which states power to the political elite and political impotency for the poor and which has as its ideal a degenerate, decadent and divisive dysfunctional political abomination known as western democracy.

If men allow jealousy and greed to distort their rationality, then they will destroy their intellectual capacity to discern that which is just and fair and thus they will have so damaged their dignity that they become no better than vegetables. But greed has no boundaries. It possesses no edges nor any definable shape. It can only be defined using established cultural practices. Since men first started setting the scope and bounds of their particular societies, those rules and regulations that restricted greed to the greedy, became symbolised in their arts and crafts thus the symbolic representation of those greedy perverts who are ever keen to gain power and possessions far in excess than that which their societies could afford or tolerate were held in check by public ridicule and that derision that naturally follows from a strong coherent cultural reaction to that well understood symbolic representation of evil.

No sooner had man become a dominant force through the enacting of his discriminatory powers of discerning good – that which is balanced – from evil – meaning unbalanced – then every type of hormonally challenged emotionally unstable intellectually subnormal person sought ways to usurp the authority that nature had granted to some and attempted to tip the scales in their favour by a ludicrous array of diversionary tactics ranging from the illogical belief that the inferiority of the perverse granted the perverse with rights and privileges and that because they were somehow numerically underrepresented that they had a god given cultural right to be represented at all. But great cultures function upon ideals that are universally applicable, that is, that apply to all those who subscribe to and are bound by the accepted rules of that culture. Though that culture may, as all natural universally applicable cultures do, state that every sentient being is of equal worth that does not and cannot imply that each and every individual has something of value and worth to give to their culture.

Indeed not many people have but as everyone is now advised that the individual self now reigns supreme and that the rights of each and every individual now far outweigh any collective rational responsibility to ensure that every person in a social structure has an equal share held in common by all the members of that society then an individualistic free for all ensues euphemistically known as a free market economy. In such economies cultures and freedoms die hand in hand with the rise of self-interested greed and the adoption of the new religions of science and consumerism.

The leaders of such societies become the embodiment of the hopes and aspirations of those disaffected and disenfranchised by that natural order of life and being the keepers of the new religions their followers must make all their declarations in their numerical and statistical language, which conveniently avoids any connection to reality, and which further empowers the state to enslave its peoples using a meaningless array of facts and figures that support their replacement cultures founded upon greed and inequality.

The state must now interfere and control every aspect of life in order that life itself can become a numerical and statistical pawn in the game of self-justifying the greed and corruption endemic in decadent democracies that sponsor state terrorism directed at anyone or anything that stands up to them.

Naturally one of the most important jobs for a true man is to protect the seeds of life and naturally it is the job of perverted politicians to ensure that this protection is state controlled.

The reason for this is that all democracies as practised are inherently decadent non-representative intellectually flawed excuses for the fortunate and debased to exercise complete control over the assets of those nations which they infest. As parasitic organisms they require a constant source of nutrients and support without actually doing anything other than to pass innumerable laws that ensure their own survival.

These parasites quickly learnt that true men were their natural enemies, and thus true men had to be rendered powerless so that that diseased organism known as western democracy could spread its malformed cancerous control over the whole planet. The aim of such a degenerate system of politics is to construct a single unitary political regime that can control this planet and its resources by the use of economic, political, military, social and industrial terrorism.

In most culturally decadent nations there is generally only one political party allowed but to fool an already sick society this is divided into two or three components, all with the same quest yet obliged to describe themselves as being 'friends to the common man' whilst attempting to whip up enthusiasm by assigning differently coloured labels to what is in effect the same old divisive political and social poisons that have rendered western societies powerless to challenge, let alone remove, their practitioners of perverted, political, parasitic injustice.

Once entrenched in their pits of slime they become too greasy to catch and they are then able to distort reality by a relentless campaign of political propaganda that miseducates to such a degree that the dysfunctional voters rubber stamp their insane requests for a single world in which everyone has an equal right to interfere with anyone or anything they care to because they believe they possess the intelligence to do so. Thus, everyone in such a situation truly believes that they have a natural right to vote for policies which have nothing to do with them and which they know nothing about.

Thus the malignant maggots of any nation who adopt an elitist and superior position founded upon and justified by a numerically distorted mandate from its culturally bankrupt and intellectually dysfunctional citizens, who are economically terrorised into adopting unnatural political allegiances to avoid the more bizarre manifestations of those blinded by avarice, pride and greed, are given what they erroneously consider to be a moral and ethical duty to stamp upon anything that would or could taint their vision of the heavenly harmonies of the one world state.

Voters therefore must be encouraged to be as selfish as their masters and to vote for that party or politician whose perversions most closely match their own. In a one world state the ideal electorate is one that is divided into isolated, dysfunctional units each with its own policy of individualistic self-fulfilment and empowerment preferably at the immediate expense to their society and ultimately at the expense of universal principles of justice and equality.

The minorities thus created are then given rights and privileges in order that their particular brand of sectarianism may be awarded that political recognition that degenerate democracies require all non-representative (and therefore underrepresented) groups to possess in order that they may be given a power and influence over the lives of others that they have no legitimate right to have and for which they lack the moral and ethical authority or the aptitude or experience to use wisely or correctly.

Thus, societies that appoint people because of some mathematical determination of their politically motivated classification as a minority group becomes a degenerate one because they have ignored their cultural heritage which asks them to behave in a proper fair and equitable manner when appointing people to positions of trust and power and who thus have a direct influence upon the lives of others.

Minorities have to be falsely created by using numerical evidence, that is by fiddling the figures, to demonstrate that certain sections of the population are either under, over, not quite or could or possibly could be not quite represented in areas in which they have no right or need to be represented in the first place.

Accordingly in nations with no cultural criteria as to what is right and proper then a numerical system is adopted but if that numerical system is made up of self-referential isolated units which end up referring to another set of self-referential isolated units, then all and everything can be self-justifiable by numbers alone. But truth cannot reside in a series of digits for numbers possess no power to delineate the quality of those objects to which they refer. If a policy is formed to be voted upon by madmen and enforced by idiots, then wherein lies those human qualities of justice and honour if that policy is to enslave others for the profit of a few?

The original concept and meaning for a democracy was that it was to provide a platform for true men to express their creative and intellectual talents in the hope of enriching their culture and their society by passing laws which would enable the collective culturalism of their society to be protected from bad practices, degenerate ideas, perverted ideals and divisive and disruptive principles.

Unfortunately, modern democracies base their meaning and justification upon a refined distortion of Greek cultural deficiencies and malpractices. This ancient, elitist riffraff introduced to the west the idea of the 'us' and 'them' type of politics. Thinking themselves near gods they concluded everyone else must be inferior and only fit for use and abuse in support of their divinely perverted practices. They introduced a hierarchical system of governing their inferiors based upon who could be the most eloquent liar.

They adopted a faulty logic of the type that distorted reality and a language to define things by syntactic definition so that whatever they said and no matter how badly they said it, it became true by definition alone.

Thus, anything could be said and because they were all educated in the same false logic whatever was said always meant something. Naturally not wishing to appear more ignorant than they were the official meaning was the intended meaning thus in politics one could talk endless drivel without fear of reproach or contradiction.

Another axiomatic essential ingredient to their mindless ramblings was an ever urgent need to go and bash somebody up, especially if others weren't listening to their self-important pronouncements, or to invade another nation to prove they could, or to simply terrorise their slaves and the population in general by indulging in outlandish acts of spartan deprivation culminating in the creation of a being somewhat less than human and thus totally unpredictable.

Naturally, these perverts who saw themselves as superhuman would prove to be ideal candidates upon which to base a whole political and social system of elitist hierarchies. Their total belief in a one world theory in which they were at the top and everything else – women, cattle, slaves and some of their more minor deities were at the bottom proved to be greatly attractive to those wishing to impose a degenerate political system in the western nations of this world.

There were those who immediately recognised that by adopting ideals that justified abusing others for profit and that ownership of common assets by dispossessing others of their natural share would lead to a system of governance which like the system it was based upon would become a self-justifying, self-relative, self-defining organisation that would define its own reality and thus would become an irremovable and near immortal structure that could take up its original quest – world domination by military, social, intellectual and economic terrorism.

Accordingly, your planet is now controlled by a bunch of divisive, sectarian bigots who are however totally unnecessary and superfluous to that order of life deemed by nature to be proper and just and that leads towards coherent and stable cultures and those worthwhile social structures that such cultures engender.

2 The New One World Order

THE NEW ONE world order, ordered by the parasitic elite, is to divide, terrorise, isolate, dispossess then enslave. One of the necessities of those decadent democracies that prostitute themselves to the highest bidder is to adopt those universal principles and thus they are forced to create conflicts by and through which they are obliged, by their paymasters, to test their weapons of terror, preferably by indiscriminately targeting the innocent.

The military cannot discriminate between the innocent and the enemy for anything and everything outside the control of those states who enforce the new world order and the globalised terror tactics required to justify it, are the enemy. The politicians are similarly duty bound to discriminate against their natural born enemy, which are true men, but they must on no account discriminate against their supporters and political allies.

Those promises made to true men to coerce them to defend the parasitic nature of the ruling democracies are conveniently forgotten when the immediate danger has passed. It is hoped that the survivors of such conflicts will be so disorientated and shell shocked that they will take no further interest in directing their justified rage at being duped yet again by those malignant maggots that infest all societies, and which are ever keen to profit from the misfortunes of others.

But perverted systems and the parasites that infest them are like thieves in that they constantly fear detection, apprehension and the ridicule and derision associated with public accountability and thus a permanent state sponsored inquisition is required in which everyone is expected to turn detective, to spy on their neighbours, to denounce the disbeliever and to make up allegations without fear of reproach, and thus deflect suspicion from themselves and their leaders.

Everyone therefore can elevate tittle-tattle, gossip and innuendo to the status of intelligent information for in the new world inquisitory ordering of reality everyone is by law equally intellectually competent to make and to assert their opinions as facts, thus the intelligence gained from such sources when mixed with the abuse of language, the fiddling of figures and that credulity with which the decadent assign to others the same perverted intentions that they harbour themselves we end up in a world where no one is safe or can legitimately challenge or refute what is said.

All forms of sanctuary are therefore forever removed from this planet and there remains no hiding place for the innocent, the harmless and the inoffensive to seek shelter from the destruction of their cultures or interference in their affairs by self-appointed sectarian bigots who parade their adoption of deformed and demented democracies as justifying the most mindless and self-interested invasion of the privacy of other peoples and nations.

The new world order of disorder is the direct result of dysfunctional democracies venting their vicious contempt for those universal cultural values that act to guard against those degenerate philosophies that arise when the interests of minorities become paramount and when the minority interests of the ruling elite dominate the culture of a particular nation.

The new world order is one in which all those qualities that made the planet a worthwhile place to be have been degraded into numerical quantities and that natural and inborn justice, known as conscience, that ensured fair play has been perverted by a meaningless array of repressive laws through the direct interference of self-appointed guardians who have impoverished the innocent by taking their land and their livelihoods and dishing out the profits to their fellow perverts.

True men understand that if one man is enslaved then we are all potential slaves. If we allow one man to be subjected, in our name, to economic, political, social or sexual terrorism then we are ourselves terrorists. As decadent political systems possess no coherent culture other than that of stupidity and greed then physical terrorism, that is, the indiscriminate destruction of life fails to have any impact upon them – it only serves their purpose.

However, what governments and global economies fear is intellectually cohesive cultures and the material alterations and interventions that naturally follow when people use their intellects to question the validity of the more obscene manifestations of greed, avarice and pride of possessions and power.

Parasitic political systems are painfully aware of the injustices that must abound to support the morally unsupportable and that distortion of reality necessary to keep the slaves slaving without hope of eternal rest.

Slavery is to live without the absolute right to food, shelter and warmth – absolute meaning without conditions. Slavery is to live under the threat of sanctions if one does not adhere to the imposition of conditions by a particular political system no matter how corrupt or elitist.

Political terrorism exists to enforce unjust rules for the unjust distribution of a nation's wealth. Slavery is to live in fear of social intervention by the state to enforce the latest proclamations of intellectually and emotionally unstable experts hired by them to create a state sponsored unnatural social and cultural society. To resist such incoherent ramblings is seen as a challenge to their usurped authority which, keenly aware of its own tentative position, forces them to tighten the screws a little further.

There is no greater terror than to inhabit a world that has become unstable and inconsistent, this lack of constancy being the result of political systems that put the interests of numerical minorities above and beyond that which could be considered fair or just to the population of a society as a whole.

As has been said intelligent useful beings are naturally limited – stupid emotionally unstable ones are not. True men by their very nature are the criteria by which all things are measured and thus in the field of cultural creativity nearly all other creatures are found to be disadvantaged when their intellectual stability and creativity is made relative to them. However the disadvantaged must never, to accord with the dogmas of the parasitic elite, must never be seen to represent the majority so a whole array of hypothetical disorders and dysfunctional diseases are engendered to enable a whole new class of numerically underrepresented disadvantaged minority sects to be established which enables an obscenely disproportionate squandering of a nation's wealth upon attempting to cure the incurable and in doing or attempting to do so the real causes of the nation's ill health are swept aside.

Thus, in sick societies individuals are assigned rights and privileges according to a numerical relationship between their dependency upon the state, their self-imposed minority status and the likelihood of them blindly supporting whichever political system panders to their needs.

Accordingly, the idea of one interconnected mass of humanity in which everyone is held together by universal cultural links which state that all existent beings are of equal worth, known as the great chain of being, must be destroyed so that each fragmentary section can claim powers and privileges to which they are not entitled and to which nature never intended or designed them to possess.

3 Protecting the Innocent

INNOCENT MEANS NOT hurting anyone, and inoffensive, that is not wishing to strikeout. One therefore considers it an outrage if harmless and inoffensive people are subjected to a reign of terror because they are blameless of any acts of self-interested aggression but who occupy a space that the culture of greed had decided ought to be stolen by immoral practices or taken by force of arms.

However, such is the cultural deficiency of those parasitic, political systems founded upon divisive and elitist principles that whole nations and their societies can be condemned to outrageous acts of aggression if their leaders fail to submit to unlawful unilateral declarations of intent to force those who disagree with the new world ordering of people about and the associated electronic slavery that condemns their cultures to become meaningless and pointless.

Accordingly all wars for economic and territorial advantage are disguised as cultural conflicts between good and evil, saint and sinner, right and wrong whereas they are simply acts of indiscriminate and mindless violence against anyone or anything that calls into question the validity of decadent and sick societies to spread their diseased and polluted democratic self-interested principles throughout other nations who prefer to live in innocence of the wonderful worlds of harmony and happiness that such exquisite regimes promise.

If a society persists in supporting offensive elitist systems of government, then who can be said to be innocent? If such diseased organisations are left unchallenged through ignorance or apathy, then who can be said to be innocent if those age-old cultural safeguards are abandoned for the individualistic self-interested greed of modernism?

The imposition of draconian rules and regulations to silence all opposition leads to those injustices that condemn the majority to unnecessary misery and hardship. If these rules and regulations are left unchallenged then who can be said not to wish others hurt or harm and therefore who can claim to be innocent?

The job of all perverted political systems is to silence opposition by miseducating their electorate, by statistical misinformation and by chopping up reality into bite sized bits of propaganda upon which their citizens grow obese and lethargic and by editing out all that may taint the delicate feelings of their inferiors by ignoring the causes that force others to undertake extreme measures to highlight those moral and ethical injustices that are being deliberately hidden.

No government, nation or peoples have the right to claim that they are innocent victims if they collude in allowing unjust, barbarous and perverted political systems to flourish at the expense and misery of others. The job of true men is to protect the innocent by attempting to right those wrongs no matter how, why or where they occur.

Naturally corrupt political systems defend themselves against such attempts at restoring equality by introducing a whole series of measures designed to pollute the minds of its electorate by empowering the scum and riff-raff to declare that decency is dead and those principles that are fit and proper in a civilised society with proper standards of behaviour are old fashioned and outdated because they curb the potential of minorities to wreak their spiteful acts of vengeance arising out of their disappointment of failing to achieve that happiness and fulfilment that was promised them by the false prophets of greed and injustice.

Those cultural safeguards that all humane societies must possess to curb those excesses that naturally arise when the interests of a minority are recognised as being worthy of universal application to the arrangement of systems of governance then if those who hold these minority views are by chance or fortune or by mindless acts of violence elevated to positions of power then those safeguards are replaced by political sectarian philosophies belonging to a particular party thus no moral or ethical or natural cure remains available to cure the diseased societies and cultures that ensue.

Those age old safeguards have been replaced by the monoform of modernism, that political sectarian philosophy which states that there is only one world, one idea, one system, one economy, one great scientific road to freedom, one type of governance – this idea allowing and encouraging all forms of mental, physical and environmental pollution for the more damaged, disorientated and sick people become the less they are inclined or able to resist the global exploitation necessary to bankroll the conversion of the world to a single form of economic and political ideology.

The new religions of science and consumerism require, in fact demand, that old fashioned cultural values are declared unscientific, unpopular and impractical as they would interfere with the obscene and disproportionate value attached to commercial interests which allows them carte blanche to behave in the most economically advantageous way irrespective of the damage they cause to the stable and coherent cultures that they encounter on their world crusade to maximise profits.

4 Computerised Culture – Fiddling the Figures

INSTEAD OF SOCIAL and political systems adapting themselves to fit the needs of reality, that is that which nature intended to be the case and those principles that form the basis of universally applicable cultures, that age old consensus as to what constitutes those rules necessary to and for the constant wellbeing of human kind, decadent western democracies cast aside this consensus and they replace that absolute and necessary constancy that is required for social integration and cultural cohesion and replace it with a perpetual reformation of the social and cultural identity and make up of their citizens.

These reformations are based upon the latest batch of the statistical evidence that was requested to contradict, support, replace or quantify another batch of evidence that evidently did not suit the promises or expectations of those in charge of converting reality into graphs, charts, percentages, numbers, degrees or probabilities of or possibilities for the fact that someone/something might, could, will, might have thought of doing something that could, might have would maybe could have affected something somewhere.

The lack of constancy thus generated by the 'it's possible' brigade is consistent with the inconsistency that naturally arises by using inconstant democratic systems which are designed to try and please everyone about everything for a finite amount of time until they use the ultimate escape clause and call upon their 'bemused by numbers' electorate to vote in another set of perverted parasites.

The major job of all decrepit, democratic, destabilising, parasitic organisations is to fiddle the figures so as to pay themselves and their pals those enormous sums necessary to buy up hovels and turn them into fashionable slums so that they can on the one hand impoverish the many by rents and taxes and dispossess the needy by keeping them languishing in trees and bus shelters or shoehorn them into those vast inhumane wastelands known as antisocial housing ghettos.

That vicious and vindictive jealousy that always arises when the superiority in numerical terms of that superior scum that wishes to float upon the wreckage of societies fragmented and divided by political and cultural incompetency if challenged by others not fitting in with their one united all pals together world ordering of everybody about makes these malignant maggots shriek with outrage that humanity is failing to fit the figures that the computerised culture of modernism states, by law, have to be complied with. Numerical equity is the name of the game and the rules of the game state that whatever the computer states is true. This must be so because the state owns the meaning not only of words but of numbers as well and as these are secret and nobody is allowed to see them in the interests of national security and to defeat those vicious and malign malcontents, armed chiefly with bicycle pumps and tubes of toothpaste, who pose such a threat to western military might.

Thus if, as in education, one sex is naturally and consistently doing better in exams get rid of exams and replace them with course work. If this still doesn't work introduce a whole array of statistical evidence that states, the reasons for this and then fiddle the figures by marking up any pupil who is underperforming through and because of some newly discovered psychological or physical disorder formerly known as laziness.

But the lazy, the incompetent, the disinterested, the subnormal, the disruptive self-interested thug, the weak, the shy, the dreamer, the clever, the devious, the simple, the innocent, the keen, the intelligent, the handsome, the ugly, the spotty, the sweet, the smelly, the gum chewer, the damaged, the anorexic, the obese, the stutterer, the dyslexic, the thief, the liar, the psychopath, the perverted, the idiot, the slow, the quick, the malign, the timid, the bold, the pubescent, the vulgar, the refined, the voluptuous, the virile, the fertile, the joker, the bully, the softy, the swot, the athlete, the duffer and so on all must be, to be equal, awarded a points system to make recompense for their parents' disgraceful behaviour in not having them genetically modified or aborted so that their offspring could fit neatly into that numerical equality of academic achievement that our masters have told us must be reached.

An education system that mixes the unmixable into a comprehensive all-inclusive state asylum in which the inmates cannot be controlled produces the elitist's dream – a miseducated socially dysfunctional electorate that will rubber stamp any absurdity and any cultural abomination and will vote into positions of power those who are their intellectual equals.

This factory fodder is further culturally disabled by being forced to subscribe to the new religions of science and consumerism and thus join the labouring train whose cultural highlights consist of growing fashionably obese whilst luxuriating in the fact that their lives have not been squandered when they discover that their hovels are worth ten times what they were yesterday.

Such is the need for perverted politicians to form a never-ending supply of zombified citizens and to avoid a proper education to those of an impressionable age, all those considered to be of an impressionable age are given rights and privileges which nature never intended them to possess. Thus, children are given rights at precisely that time of life when they are designed to be educated in the culture of their country as to what rights are right for them to possess once they have been educated into being able to either accept or reject those cultural contracts necessary for the efficient and equitable functioning of their society.

Thus, for the state to assign rights at the wrong time leads to the young abusing those rights because they are too young to understand that once accepted, they lose the right to choose their rights relative to their culture. Accordingly, they turn to cultures of their own which cannot be controlled and measured by mathematics.

To accord with the new world order everything must be measured. Satellites spend all day photographing every inch of the planet, every house, every tree. Everything must be objectified so that it can form a number or be a number so that it can have a numerical relationship with whatever reality the one world order has chosen for today. Quantity has replaced quality. Those great wars that were fought to preserve the quality of life in the west can never be repeated for a new standard now flies over decadent cultures – quantity of life replaces quality of life.

This new mathematical measure of how happy we all are now that the latest political parasites have spun their webs of wonder is controlled by our governors to ensure that we have no means of knowing how and when they fiddle the figures to accord with what was promised and how those promises can be shown statistically to have been fulfilled.

Accordingly, the greatest holocaust since records began is being daily entrenched in the lives of human kind by the ripping out and burning of living flesh so that the perfect ratio of slaves and production targets may be met with the least cost in financial and numerical terms to the nation.

When the irrational is made rational a race of peoples is spawned whose fetish for figures zombifies them to such an extent that their cultures become entirely based upon numerical relationships thus a work of creativity can only have a meaning and value relative to its worth in a numerical interpretation of the number of units currently used as currency that the culture defines as creditworthy. Thus, to be culturally aware, creative and have meaning and value all modern cultures must to prove how creditable they are live on credit and not on value. A whole new array of minorities then appear who accrue to themselves rights and privileges far beyond that which is proper, balanced or fair for just because they are both numerical and cultural minorities their interests should not be doubled numerically when the quality of those interests is of no cultural value.

In a well-balanced and cohesive culture where everyone is considered to be of equal worth this does not and cannot mean that everyone's opinion or creativity or occupation is of equal value to the quality of their community. However, as they are of equal worth their value in numerical terms must be respected for all stable societies have an absolute need for an extensive and diverse range of members each with an essential, though differing, task.

In sick societies that maintain obscenely divisive, disproportionate, numerical rewards for those who are merely doing their allotted share for no other reason than that is the job or occupation that nature has best fitted them to serve their society, the society becomes unbalanced when everyone wishes to become that person, literally to become that occupation regardless to the cost to their intellectual integrity and the loss of humanity that may result.

If the reward in numerical terms accords with the promise of the parasitic maggots who promote such schemes, then it is of no relevance how many were trampled down by the stampede for success nor how many faces were disfigured as they were stood upon because now every individual has been given the right to be as equally degraded and obnoxious as another.

Further as decency is now dead so must personal privacy be derided and discarded so that the new state sponsored inquisition and its henchmen in the media can spy and pry without fear of reproach because like every tree, house and wall we are now objects to be measured and interfered with because we are in fact, as soon as we are given our equal rights, public property and the public therefore have a right to believe whatever our measurers tell them.

Thus, as public property whoever measures us can state any number of falsehoods but as long as these lies are numerical it is of no consequence for numbers simply refer to probabilities or possibilities that whatever is said truly reflects the degree of malice of the informant and the expected degree of decadence of the victim.

We no longer, we are told, have the stains of original sin but our sins have to be original to merit our inclusion into the hierarchies of politically perverse organisations. In a nation freed from those cultural restraints that arrest the decline into decadence and which curb degenerate behaviour and conduct by making cultural contracts binding a dysfunctional and confused electorate are by law entitled to vote no matter how intellectually or morally damaged and thus you can only get out what you put in.

If the result is a nation led by intellectually subnormal parasitic maggots and you then combine their rational inabilities with a fetish for figures and an adoration of science and technology which has given them uncontrolled access to destructive weapons, then who is safe?

They then gang up together and feel free to terrorise anything or anybody that is statistically a threat – thus they become the world's true terrorists – those uncontrollable diseased organisms driven by greed and self-interest who are free to use and abuse numerical relationships to justify acts of gross injustice. They use this form of terrorism to maintain their dominance and to fulfil the dream of all democratic dictatorships, that is, there is only one world (two different and differing worlds is strictly forbidden), no just one (the ultimate numerical relationship) and it is ours – not yours – ours.

Well, what is the point? Well, there isn't one unless true men use their rationality, their intelligence and their creativity in order to return life to its natural course. The true men of history are those truly creative creatures who understood that great cultural revolutions must be founded upon the honour, dignity, self-reliance and creativity of man.

True men must therefore use their creativity to establish worthwhile and universally acceptable cultures – facts, figures and statistics are those artless and easily distorted creations by which the inferior attempt to chain true men down – but it is by art and then by culture that all men will ultimately be free.

5 Art and Culture

WHAT IS ART? Art is the skilful interpretation of an idea or an emotion. The skill involved in making concepts and ideas accessible to others is not by nature granted to everyone thus to be entitled to the name of artist one must demonstrate the ability to not only create pleasing objects but also to make their meaning and thus their significance readily accessible.

Accordingly there can be no cultural significance to objects so abstruse and ill-defined that their use appears limited to fostering a belief amongst the ill-bred that they must be of value because others are prepared to pay large sums of a nation's commonwealth in order to purchase rationally meaningless artefacts and then to house them in public trivia warehouses, guarded night and day lest some intruder or malcontent disturbs the exquisite ordering of their enigmatic combination of body parts and double discount store emulsion mixed and applied employing that ubiquitous style reserved for the uncontrollable and the unaccountable.

If political systems cannot be controlled nor made accountable, then why should those who purport to possess the intellectual integrity and skill to convert their ideas into hylomorphic forms which have a meaning and relevance beyond that incestuous clique of self-congratulatory hypocrites who claim to possess superhuman powers that enable them to untangle one set of moronic meanings from another.

But the meaningless morons of modernism are subsidised by the state to inflict as much cultural and intellectual damage as possible for then those who cannot aspire to comprehend the irrelevancies of the incompetent must be made to feel inadequate and thus inferior to the task of creating and supporting their own artistic endeavours and thus eventually their own independent cultures.

A society that produces artists with the skill, intellectual capacity and moral integrity to produce accessible works that can demonstrate those universal qualities that make life worth living, that guard against the adoption of malodorous practices and that demonstrate the need for social cohesion and the defeat of individualism for the sake of society as a whole will eventually through proper and selective education produce a coherent and worthwhile culture.

If a culture degenerates into a political democratic dictatorship which relies upon and advocates using slavery and elitism which is supported by greed and military terrorism then its artists will be as elusive, decadent and as culturally unaccountable as their paymasters.

Accordingly decadent cultures can be identified by their painfully bizarre attempts to cater to and for the self-satisfaction of each individual by blatant imagery of perverse and degenerate relationships at one end of the social spectrum and obscure, unavailable and mysterious tripe at the other.

However, a false sense of culture must be generated to add some excitement to the dull and drab days of the slaves to consumerism. Accordingly, a popular culture is invented in which the words, colours and sounds of everyday life are condensed, chopped up into bite size bits, speeded up and mixed up with the bizarre imaginations of various writers and delivered at maximum colour and full volume so that everyday people may watch everyday people portraying their meaningless lives via a two dimensional electronic image in their meaningless and miserable hovels.

It is the fact that most lives are so culturally poor and morally unsatisfactory that remorselessly forces the slaves of the new religions to seek sanctuary in property and possessions and when this fails, they gawp at and dream of far away places with villas, sunshine and freedom. This never ending and futile quest for cultural and thus spiritual enrichment is only eternal and unobtainable because the first and greatest necessities of life have to be acquired at such a cost to health, personal and interpersonal relationships as well as time that no time remains for people to understand what the purpose of being human is.

To be a slave is to live without any absolute rights. An absolute right means 'granted without conditions'. We have, all of us – every single human, have at the moment of conception an absolute right granted by nature to exist. Nature in its wisdom then decides our lifespan, the reason for our existence and then grants us all that is necessary for each individual being to fulfil their natural born purpose. Nature grants us a planet, food, water and shelter. It provides an order of life in which every person is assigned to a task for which they are by nature best suited. It does not hide from us but gives freely all that it possesses in a balanced and just manner. For the ills and fevers, it gives us its opiates. In return it asks only one thing and one thing only. It asks us to avoid greed. It furnishes man with an awareness of what greed is. It is said that the original sin of man was to be tempted to obtain from life more than life could give and thus when tempted by others to be superior to nature itself he became aware of himself and immediately understood that to amend for his pride and greed he must sacrifice life itself in the pursuit of creating cultures that had at their very heart the idea that all creatures are of equal worth and that none should ever adopt a position of superiority over another in their quest for distinction.

The messages that nature gives us are simple and clear. We are designed by it to understand what it is telling us. Naturally there are those conceived into this world that cannot or wilfully refuse to understand those messages. Nature grants everyone that freedom of choice necessary to determine their own fate but it also grants some of its creatures the ability to create strong and vibrant cultures which can guide the unsure and make outcasts of the greedy and avaricious.

There is a saying, 'No cross – No crown', meaning if one is never tested then one can never have success. Nature has therefore created worlds in abundance for those who pass those tests that this world creates for us. One of the first great essentials to even discovering what tests await us is to be free from the parasitic practices of others so that we have time to discover and to reflect upon the purpose of why we, the way we are, exist at all.

Once enslaved, therefore, into an intellectually illegitimate elitist and dictatorial degenerate democracy one is powerless to act even when one is forced to witness gross acts of barbarism.

One therefore has to start asking questions. Can any human being in such a society state, 'I am not to blame – I am innocent' if they see their neighbour's house being bulldozed and then them being dispossessed of their land and then do nothing?

If they see someone poisoning the land and destroying crops and they then support the polluter by buying their produce can they then state, 'It's nothing to do with me.'

All worthwhile philosophies and the cultures from which they arise state that existence is one great chain of being, each person, animal and object forming an indispensable link between nature, each other and this planet so that its bounty and wealth may diffuse equally throughout the whole, without distinction.

Naturally it is the job of any political system founded upon a faulty adaptation of a faulty democratic system to use hypothetical scientific and technological advances (though in which direction is not clear) to break up the idea of that great uniting chain into isolated sectarian units which are further divided by repressive and unjust laws into secularised factions.

These factions finding themselves lonely and isolated reform into either minority interest groups or dominant political movements both of which tend to look like, sound like and have the moral and intellectual capacity of a union between the rancid cabbage water of muddled thinking and the grotesque deformity of living by numbers. This is because if universal cultures die such groupings possess no criteria of what the proper way to re-link humanity is back together nor the correct sequence or ordering of links.

Once lost the order of life can only be reconstituted by true men reasserting that authority granted by nature to reassemble that great chain of being by them creating new cultures and then educating their offspring in those philosophies that arise from those cultures.

Decadent states and their dysfunctional political systems therefore, if they are to survive as parasitic entities, must keep their citizens isolated from such a chain and they therefore encourage them to form individualistic cliques, sects and minority groupings each with its own rules and codes of conduct so that their societies lack cohesion and thus can be manipulated with ease.

When a society becomes divisive and secularised with self-interested individualism sponsored by greed as its main raison d'être, then it becomes a sick society. However, that foul layer of scum that naturally forms upon the surface of such fetid futility (because they view life through distorted goggles and rely upon mathematical interpretations of reality) appear to themselves to be visibly above the rest of sunken humanity and thus this superiority must entitle them to a wildly disproportionate share of their nation's wealth. The more decadent a nation the more disproportionate the division of wealth.

The term used to describe the decline of civilised societies into dysfunctional secular societies is known as progress. In the two-dimensional world of the culturally dormant no direction to this progress can be given, it merely implies that society is constantly moving even if it is only circling around itself in despair.

Fortunately, the statistics clearly demonstrate that the more others are dispossessed and then starve to death the faster we as a nation are progressing towards becoming a modern society. Naturally this must mean 'better' but 'better' for whom? Modern means 'of the present' – fortunately it does not mean permanent – well not yet. The whole quest and thrust of defective democracies is to ensure 'modern' means 'permanent' irrespective of how their permissive political dogmas lead to the cultural and physical poverty of their one and only world.

It is the job of true men to create cultures that demonstrate to others how one being ought to relate to another and to illustrate how the isolation and interference with even one link in a chain can adversely affect the whole. True men are thus advised and educated to see not only part of the puzzle but are uniquely granted the intellectual ability to glimpse the whole picture.

It is the job of science to see only one piece of the puzzle at a time, separated, isolated and interfered with without any idea of how that separation and isolation may adversely affect every other link in the chain. Science cannot function any other way for that is what science means. Nature has taken untold ages to lock up its venom – science has just started, and the pollutants already released will last more or less indefinitely.

True men have been granted the intellectual capability to understand those ideals, systems and the political processes necessary to make living worthwhile and culturally productive. They understand what means are necessary to uphold those values and practices that make life meaningful and thus they have a duty to uphold their culture and that civilised behaviour that those cultures require to uphold the moral and ethical standards necessary for fair and just societies.

Global political and economic systems are given the duty to destroy all civilisations that do not subscribe to the one world theory. This one world theory is advocated and taught throughout the west and forms the basis of modern political thinking.

The popularity of the one world philosophy is owing to the ease with which it gives its adherents an excuse for indulging in acts of extreme violence and stupidity because the theory itself cannot be challenged directly by using any rational or intellectual methods because the theory itself, as a coherent, useful, reasonable, justifiable and beneficial concept, does not in fact exist in any objectified cultural form. It is simply the invention of the elitists based upon the defective philosophies of those inept fashionable thinkers that were spawned as a result of the industrial revolution. As the world was gearing up to accommodate the technical and scientific advances necessary to keep pace with the possibilities of power that an abundance of coal, iron and steel made then it was thought necessary to update and revolutionise philosophical and cultural attitudes and perceptions so that human nature could be modified to accommodate the dictates of modernisation.

Human nature unfortunately is composed of bits and pieces that cannot be tampered with directly thus a particularly vicious type of wretch was spawned whose whole purpose in existence was to either amuse themselves with propounding theories of hypothetical insignificance regarding the functioning of the mind or by an inhuman and tortuous destruction of living creatures in an attempt to discover how those bits and pieces functioned. Ever wishing to be trendy the philosophers whose astounding vagueness in compiling any useful and artful discipline to enable and empower others to make balanced, rational and productive choices so as to be in a position to enrich their cultures and societies tried vainly to keep pace with the products of mass production, and the policies of those politicians who based their pronouncements upon the psychoanalytic procrastinations of the psychoanalysts who were always ready to take to flights of fancy but were careful to couch them in the 'it's possible', 'maybe', 'could do', 'just might' category of non-essential nonsense.

Accordingly, as then, as now, no one could be held to account for politicians and other intellectually challenged emotionally, unstable, dysfunctional, interfering busy bodies never take the blame for their own stupid actions.

How then are true men to take charge and to make sense of a world that has become unstable and fragmented so that it may be reconstructed without using the divisive and distorted democratic principles that aim to make the world into a single planet controlled and operated by an insane elite?

The defence mechanism used by debased democratic systems is to enshrine as many written laws protecting their system from legitimate and justified challenges as possible. The original purpose of laws were to ensure the equal distribution of that wealth held in common and granted by nature between not only those who could immediately benefit from the world's natural bounty but all existent creatures that were held together by that great natural chain known as humanity.

Thus, the great law courts write above themselves that they exist to protect the poor. Yet what can be designed more catastrophically than western legal systems that base justice upon ill conceived, ill formulated, misunderstandable, irrelevant and absurdly complex laws formulated in an archaic language and made absolutely powerless to protect anybody but the elite by a ridiculous concatenation of subordinate clauses which are tacked on to try and make them appear to do justice to those who, in decadent societies, always end up dispossessed.

A whole array of self-serving exegetist is spawned who delights in confounding the weary and weak by stirring the inconsequential mud of adversarial litigation and who become ecstatic at the thought of prostituting themselves in a grubby attempt to impoverish their clients by abusing their time in an attempt to extract the greatest amount of recompense that the system will permit.

But when one seriously considers that the laws that these wretches have to deal with are those self-serving ideals expounded by the parasitic elite to enforce their own morbid view of human nature and thus like all cultural delinquents they while away their pitiful lives in morally squalid gothic reformatories ever keen to empower themselves and their henchmen with the latest flights of fancy, statistically and scientifically endorsed as reality, which they use to terrorise their own citizens and any others as the mood takes them.

A cycle of slavery and cultural deprivation are the necessary attendant results of such perverse systems. Once caught up in such systems humanity is debased to a meaningless mathematical relationship that attempts to quantify man's value solely upon the degree to which he can enrich himself at the expense of others.

Laws need not be complex, nor should they require advocates. Proper laws simply require the relationship between logic and language to be understood. True logic (not those syllogistic absurdities so favoured by the ancients) and the use of the English Language based upon its prescriptive definitions of what is to be the case, that is what is to be considered 'real' would then enable all laws to be formulated as positive prescriptive commands to do something and not those negatory prescriptive commands not do something. As soon as you request anybody not to do something it is almost inevitable that they will. As soon as you request anybody to do something it is almost inevitable that they won't bother but at least evil is to a great extent avoided.

Thus commands 'Thou shalt not' become 'Thou shall' become 'Thou should' become 'You should'. Culture states that which you should do to occupy your time to enrich yourself and your society. Philosophy demonstrates 'how' you could and then culture explains 'why' you should. It is at this very point of transition between 'how' you could help and 'why' you should help that the spirituality of man as more than mere animal enters the frame of reference. All living creatures possess souls, it is just that man's state of awareness gives him a domination over all living creatures because he has a choice between good or bad intentions. Only the soul of man is aware of what those intentions are, and it is only the soul of man that is judged. One cannot reprove a one-legged dwarf from failing to qualify for the pole vault event at the Olympics if they intended only to bring honour to their fellow dwarfs, yet you would be entitled to suggest a more fitting sport.

But what are then the intentions behind the 'one world and its ours theory' of decadent, degenerate democracies? Are they merely honourable in their wish that all of human kind should possess an equal share of and in this planet and that all existent creatures have an absolute right to life from the moment of conception and an absolute right to food, shelter and warmth combined with an absolute right to be free from aggression and interference by busybodies and an everlasting commitment by a league of nations not to subject them to military, social, sexual, political and economic terrorism?

One may believe that the true intentions of all degenerate elitist political systems founded upon numerical and self-appointed superiority is to control all living creatures for their own profit.

This ideal once entrenched into the political life of nations is like a cancer which cannot be treated or removed without the death of civilised societies.

The idea itself is protected by the number one catch that is endemic to all sick societies led by perverted politicians and overseen by a degenerate culture of self-interest and greed.

This catch numero uno states that democracies can only be removed by democratic means and that those democracies that are to be removed by democratic means decide what democratic means are allowed to remove those democracies. In other words, 'if we don't like your politics you're banned.'

Thus, the one world theory not only states that not only is there only one world and it's ours, but it also further states that everything in that world must accord with the one world only theory or it becomes a proscribed organisation. Thus, the one world elitist political perverts describe what they consider to be a threat irrespective of how innocuous or harmless that perceived threat is or could be.

Thus, a one-legged dwarf with a particularly sharp pole would pose a significant threat to the nuclear arsenals of the decadent west and its sycophantic allies.

These psychos are ever keen to distort their own democracies even further so that they accord with the cultural criteria that underpin all degenerates that of dispossessing others and using a misplaced sense of superiority and self-importance in keeping it that way.

If one is born into decadent political systems that give you the right to vote for decadent political parties who enact decadent laws, then how is one to know any better? If one is born into a political system that allows anyone to vote upon any subject then how is one to know if they understand the issues, if they are capable of making a reasonable choice or if they are simply voting 'cos they like the look of the candidate's jacket?

In strong, coherent and cohesive cultures with clearly defined and accessible works that encapsulate the hopes, aspirations and direction that a society wishes to take and that permits those fundamental rights for existence to be enshrined in its laws those issues that require the will of the people to be expressed in numerical terms cannot in themselves endanger the individual and universal cultural rights and freedoms of the electorate. The issues that democracies deal with, that is, what is proper for them to put to universal suffrage should be naturally restricted to the processes required for the day to day running of a nation. They have and could not have any legitimate right to alter or interfere with those fundamental rights that are necessary for all living creatures to survive with decency and integrity upon the face of this planet.

But the whole purpose of a parasite is to live off others and encumber them in difficulties and to bring pain and misery. These culturally diseased organisms are designed to withstand the most forceful attempts to remove and burn them. They cling to their positions with a tenacity that defies reason itself. They are painfully aware that without a host to prey upon and an arsenal of noxious and self-destructive weapons they would be cast aside and destroyed.

The great scientific and technological revolutions have been granted to all so that true democracies may emerge through and by the use of electronic accountability. Numbers are not designed for any other use but to allow mankind to make themselves accountable to each other and to nature. In a true democracy with true accountability and a truly fundamental system of individual rights and cultural responsibilities all those ideas and methods of handling those ideas and concepts necessary to maintain a just and fair society would form those disciplines that all the citizens of that society would be required to understand and would further be required to demonstrate their capacity to remember and use those cultural gifts in a worthwhile and meaningful way.

If there is only one world then it is ours, not theirs. 'Ours' in the sense that every penny that you share with another in the commonwealth of this world can and should be accounted for. Living by numbers will become living through numbers these numbers being freely available to all so that all may see if all is well.

6 The Natural Order of Intellectual Life

IT HAS TAKEN all of time to order life upon this planet into a viable and useable form yet at that very moment when man became the first truly rational creature capable of reigning supreme his very existence became threatened by that greed and jealousy that arises when others not so well endowed with similar abilities took that road which whispers the age old lie that if we eat from the tree of science which bears the fruit of knowledge of power and destruction then those who eat will become invincible, immortal and indestructible.

The superiority in physical terms thus gained would allow these malcontents to rule the world and allow that vindictive spite against nature and their fellow creatures for not granting them the intellectual capacity to become like true men(and be fair, honest, just and creative) to be unleashed without restraint. This glitch in creation no matter the cause has condemned countless creatures to a life of pain and suffering, misery and slavery, poverty and chaos.

Great empires sprang up to enslave the world and great wars were fought between those who protested at those universal cultural values that were created to try and heal the rift between mankind and its spiritual destiny. These empires and wars which stained the planet were the offspring of decadent democracies and cultures that rejected the concept of an all-embracing universal culture. Accordingly, the participants were protestant nations each one subjugated by degenerate dictatorial democracies who owed their existence to that greed and avarice which enslaves others under the banner of freedom and self-determination to a futile and pointless existence.

All so called democracies are in fact no more than numerical dictatorships since they can never be removed other than by physical extinction or numerical extinction. However, as they possess all the weapons for ensuring the mass extinction of their enemies, that leaves numerical extinction. But if nobody voted they would still remain. If everybody voted they would still remain. If everybody voted to 'Remove the elitist parasitic scum' they would still remain in their bunkers until their allies in the one world state came and took over the country and all opposition was deported to some wasteland

and left there to rot. However to avoid the expense and trouble they have found it more convenient to make those promises necessary for each and every one of us to fulfil our newly discovered scientifically enhanced destinies which promise the banishment of all ills and diseases through an intensive programme of health and education, and unlimited financial rewards for those who will demonstrate a complete disrespect for the quality of life in their quest to maximise profits.

Thus, a loyal band of supporters is established with each political party pitching its patter and promises at a particular section of society so that hopefully it will outdo another political party and scrape home even if it does so by a few votes. However, it is irrelevant which set of malignant parasites presides over a nation for they share a complete contempt for anyone or anything that would suggest natural and simple methods of alleviating a great deal of unnecessary suffering and misery.

If one suggested free living space, they would suffer apoplectic shock. If one suggested that for a small fraction of the resources wasted upon those self-inflicted disorders that manifest themselves through the degenerate lifestyles of their sick societies one could ensure everyone could be given a safe refuge, then they would send the new world inquisition round to see you.

But such basic provisions as factory constructed shelters slotted into soundproof and secure concrete frames would seriously threaten the economies of those parasitic organisms which have educated their followers into a belief system founded upon a physical, inherent and natural class system appointed by their god to oversee their world. Thus wishing to adhere to their new earthly religions of greed, avarice and consumerism their ultimate aim in life is to acquire as many loathsome hovels as possible, preferably with barking dogs and stuck in the worst area possible and then let them out at exorbitant rents so that they can fulfil that dream that lingers in the heart of every true blue decadent democrat, that of being a slum landlord.

If such societies find that they cannot rent their hovels because they have inadvertently slaughtered too many of the unborn then vast numbers must be imported or their slums will lie empty and rotting away and thus they will be unable to drive round the corner in their eight wheel car to their local junk shop to talk in lardy dah voices about what piece of tacky trash little Johnny would like when he returns from his sure to start badly indoctrination classes. True means literally straight, not devious. No politicians are straight towards their electorate. Why should they be – it would be a contradiction in terms. It is the duty of true men to remove such pestilential parasites from the political and economic systems of all nations.

Their intentions are to perpetuate those corrupt systems that ensure that the wealth of a nation, its resources and its infrastructure including food, shelter and warmth are prostituted to the highest bidder.

A market economy means exactly that – humans are simply enslaved creatures who are forced to parade themselves around a marketplace for anybody to bid for their time.

Not only are we open to be used and abused by anybody who cares to buy our time but so is our land, our homes and our possessions. In a global one world economic system anyone can also buy and possess anything they care to. They are free to abuse and misuse, pollute and pervert. There are no cultural codes of conduct left to control that vindictive spite that the greedy exact on themselves and others. The two latest great wars fought from greed and hatred and a universal wish to be the ultimate one world dictator was an economic battle to inherit the right to control this planet and its resources. But the greedy and the perverted not only despise and hate those that they murder and dispossess they despise each other with such an intensity that even the losers in such conflicts if they are seen to be benefiting and profiting from their own destruction by rising from the ashes and creating economic wealth their self-appointed victors fly into a paralytic shock which mutates into a form of paraplegia which is taken up by its traumatised citizens and its henchmen in the media.

Eventually aware that their own brutal and disreputable behaviour has not reaped the rewards to which they feel themselves entitled the original intellectual dysfunctioning caused by the shock of seeing the vanquished rise again ensures that the high point of their culture becomes a campaign of institutionalised remembrance days with repeated showing of archaic court jesters goose stepping towards world domination through military might.

By fiddling the figures and perverting prices the elite become numerically rich though not wealthy and thus can hide their sick societies and devalued culture behind a plethora of phoney statistics and the polished smiles of the photogenic that are daily paraded through the papers in various degrees of decadence in order to demonstrate to the working man that all's well with the world.

In a nation that permits the import of large numbers of slaves and encourages anyone from anywhere to buy our land, houses and natural wealth and resources and then give them the right to control where and how we live whilst condemning untold numbers to live in squalor and misery then true men have an overriding moral and cultural duty to remove those persons responsible and make them accountable to their peoples.

We are told that the free market economies of the world generate great wealth and that is why they are the rich nations of the world. So where are these riches? Are they used to provide food, shelter and warmth for human kind? Do we live in pollution free secure homes possessing absolute rights and protection from interference from poverty, the state or their henchmen in the media?

Decadent states are proud to squander vast sums upon meaningless military hardware and even greater sums on an even more meaningless and indefinable concept known as health. In cultures that understand these issues health becomes definable by and through those philosophies that arise from allowing an intelligent – not an economic approach to good living.

Health means whole and in its original meaning 'the whole person' and by inference their environment. Accordingly great emphasis must be put upon the mental health of individuals for it has been long understood that physical health is directly affected by maintaining the brain free from disturbances. That which most disturbs the brain is stress, that tensioning of the nervous system and its control centre through those fears and anxieties that living in culturally decadent inconstant dictatorial societies in which anyone or anything are given the lawful right to interfere with and make demands upon anyone that they want to.

However, the perverted politicians of decadent democracies would rather bulldoze their cities to the ground than provide, as an absolute right, those basics of life that are essential for people to lead stress free constructive lives in which they are freed from those everyday stresses that free market economies impose upon them. Fair and just cultures understand that people need time and mental space and thus spiritual integrity to enrich themselves and their cultures. If the mind is full of today it has no chance or spare capacity to give to tomorrow.

All evil cultures recognise the need to instil fear and terror and deny absolute rights to its slaves and drones. This is not only an essential requirement to keep people from questioning the validity of their existence but also to make their supporters pliable and subservient to the demands that the state makes upon them to be the eyes and ears of the new world inquisition.

Thus, throughout the world this denial to an absolute and natural right to the basics of life both in physical and mental terms is an inbuilt essential for all self-appointed dictatorial democracies to exert their malignant intentions upon all who fall foul of their vicious onslaught upon the innocent. It is the job of true men to defend the innocent – no matter the cost.

7 Protecting the Seeds of Life

WHEN CURRENT POLITICAL thinking slavishly follows a scientific method of evaluating the worth of an individual by assigning numerical units to that organism's relative worth to themselves and that society which they represent then if those political thinkers decide to disrupt the balance which nature provides to ensure an equal distribution of those skills and abilities that coherent and strong societies require to maintain strong and unified cultures then societies and cultures begin to degenerate toward social structures founded upon individual rights no matter the price to social and cultural cohesion.

Nature long ago decided what would be the perfect blend of perfections and deformities, the one to ensure great cultures, the other to prevent pride. It also saw the advantage of each individual being a mixture, a well-balanced human, no matter how disabled, for it was known that no matter what little one had to offer in return it would or could be in just proportion to that received. It is therefore incumbent upon those who receive the most to give the most they can afford and those who receive the least to give what they can afford. But those with the most cannot know what is expected of them without a strong cultural inheritance of what constitutes fair play. Thus, in societies that possess weak and sickly cultures there are no readily accessible and publicly understood guidelines and those pathetic cultural weeds that have not the standing or authority to resist those blasts of greed and self-interest of the fortunate and the powerful thus wilt into further insignificance. Accordingly, those born with most keep the most.

An elite group is thus spawned who receive no worthwhile cultural inheritance and their education is either in the classical falsehoods of the culturally inept and the intellectually perverted or they are subjected to a comprehensive system which has never even heard of cultural beliefs other than those displayed on the menus of their favourite takeaway.

Thus, the elite are cast adrift from the great cultural bonds that signify the degree of civility that nature and life require to avoid being subjected to perverse and improper interference with its natural functioning.

But the elite are further contaminated with those obsequious, sycophantic malcontents who wish to appear fortunate and blessed by becoming associated with fame and power by making themselves appear indispensable in apportioning the wealth of their master's whilst appropriating an obscenely disproportionate share unto themselves.

Such is the intensity of the self-interest and mutual dependency thus generated that a class of elitist parasitic and symbiotic organisms is engendered who, having no healthy, worthwhile or honourable method of living, begin to decay and degenerate into a festering and malignant hierarchy that seeks only to bring all others down to their miserable and lonely level. These hierarchies therefore seek every opportunity to invade, dominate and ultimately destroy.

The first act of destruction is therefore to destroy life itself. To achieve this, they require the services of an inquisitorial system of such might that it requires full use of all those resources that the state can muster. This new inquisition is ordered to seek and destroy all and any opposition to their malignant intents.

This new world inquisition states that there is only one world and one form of government. It further states that a one world dictator must approve of all and every political party and movement. There is no such thing as privacy. Everybody everywhere is deemed to be up to no good and thus the inquisition and its henchmen are permitted to breach all and any rules of civilised conduct.

In those sick societies which grow daily more deranged there are always those who clamour for notice and attention from their masters and are thus advised by their feeble cultures to become gossip mongers and to elevate the tittle-tattle they have gleaned by interfering in the lives of others to the status of well thought out and evidently justifiable prepositions of reality known as 'intelligent information' or simply 'intelligence'.

This new inquisition is the means by which the tarted-up religions of greed and consumerism are held above ridicule and scorn. As privacy and decency are now dead everyone living in a diseased democracy now belong to the state. Thus, the state in return promises to protect its citizens from terrorism in order that it will be free to terrorise them itself.

The new inquisition and the new religions are now empowered by and through a free market economy (which is anything but free other than to plunder) and the use of the numerical sciences to rearrange the natural order of life. Everything we now do is risky. Everything and every action is now measured in financial terms and thus the influence of numerical financial risk assessment agencies has spread like wildfire. Insurance companies can now therefore dictate our social structuring and our cultural habits because the whole of our culture is now based upon fear and fear of litigation by mindless morons, fear of loss for what little we have and worst of all the ultimate fear that the state in attempting to become the final arbiter does in fact become the final arbiter.

To believe that the state as final judge and jury is impartial to the needs of its most vociferous advocates when confronted by the poor and dispossessed thus numerically inferior is a matter of personal conscience.

All true men must realise that the state is now free to terrorise its own population but as it has abandoned shooting them or hanging them has turned to social engineering. Their first act is to remove any form of sanctuary. The days when people could hide in churches and monasteries have long gone, these being destroyed in a vicious fit of temper by some cash strapped oaf who thought himself nearer God than the rest of the world put together. As with all reformations of the natural order only fear and destruction are the result. But these reformists would quail at the thought that some hapless citizen was even left with a twig to shield themselves with for naturally the twig would be owned by somebody probably a local council or nature reserve and would require planning permission and being a desirable country residence commanding fine views of the local tip would therefore be considered in the upper band for the imposition of exorbitant local taxations these being desperately required for the new gold leaf wallpaper in the council offices.

Nobody, no thing, no idea, no word, no attempt at anything anywhere is now beyond their interference. Everything now has a value. Even those worthless slums built in vast numbers in the latter part of the 20ᵗʰ century have a value so if nobody can be found to buy them then they must be boarded up and then demolished lest someone inadvertently sleeps in them.

We are no longer free from state impositions. The importune nature of life now dictates that we pay close attention to the needs of our parasitic governors and their allies by having a duty to be ever alert to the flotsam and jetsam of life (in case it is explosive) and to spy upon our neighbour (in case they are explosive). Thus, the inquisition can litigate using laws enacted by and for the parasitic to ensure their survival in that eternal sanctuary of decadent democratic dictatorships whilst the poor and dispossessed live in constant fear not of some exterior threat but only that they may be further impoverished by that abuse of language and logic that accompanies all unjust prosecutions for profit.

This form of cultural pollution clogs up the courts, whose origins were based upon the poor laws, yet not only are the poor forced to watch the inept ineptly defend them by using a language that they do not fully understand, to defend using laws that they do not fully comprehend, which have been enacted by a legislature that is oblivious to the logic of justice and goodness, they are further condemned to the pollutants of noise, mental disease and a whole unnecessary array of chemical cocktails that the state believes essential in keeping the consumer consuming.

The long-term survival of that species known as human depends upon what true men do now. If corrupt political systems are permitted to pollute our food and water, our courts and our cultures and then are permitted to stand by and watch the wealth of a nation be distributed according to some bigoted sectarian, divisive doctrines then we will return to being wild irrational animals, with a culture founded upon greed, and where the only response to justified opposition is a mindless violence culminating in a vicious and unending persecution by the state inquisition and their lapdogs in the media.

Should true men let sick societies fiddle the figures to prove that they are not really that sick after all? Or let them continue to rip the living flesh from creatures in order to promise to prolong the lives of the old and afflicted who simply wish to die in befuddled peace at home in their own private sanctuary.

Should true men watch perverted democratic ideas founded upon archaic distortions of reality ruin societies and cultures both at home and abroad when science and technology has given man the electronic means to deconstruct antiquated and corrupt institutions and replace them with proportionate systems of governance based upon those universal concepts which make life worth living.

It would be the beginning of turning true men into free men – those independent, creative creatures who cannot be used and abused for the profit of others and who are essential to make, defend and enrich their cultures.

8 The Meaning of Words

TRUTH IS WHAT is real, and reality is dependent upon how things are presented to us. If we are not present at an event, then we are dependent upon what others may care to tell us or show us of that event. If one therefore lives in a culture of secrecy founded upon a longstanding tendency to cheat and lie and to break every promise or treaty ever made between that culture and another then a feeling of doubt and scepticism regarding what is said and what is done would naturally or should naturally arise when such cultures state that their past conduct was honourable, necessary and justifiable.

Many western cultures are founded upon avarice and greed combined with a total lack of respect for all verbal and written agreements and must therefore change the meaning of words by making them relative to the present and the future and to disconnect them from their past meanings.

To this end the term 'modern' is used to infer the here and now. Thus, the word 'now' now excuses all past crimes. But if this word is linked to the rate of change necessitated by and the disruption caused through the state's need to keep its economic prisoners in a state of permanent anxiety, fear and confusion regarding local, national and world events then a false sense of order and improvement and change for the better must be generated because if one set of parasites fails to convince their submissive supporters that all is well when it obviously isn't, and the standard 'that was then not now' fails to impress then to generate a belief that things can and will change for the better simply call another election. Thus the word 'now' implies a new system of cultural awareness that has at last reformed the political elite and they have suddenly seen the light and in their new found humility have discovered what honour and integrity mean and in an act of repentance they are going to their electorate with open and honest policies that will change their bad old ways and that they will deliver a manifesto that will ensure justice, fairness and equality for all.

This daydream of a decent democracy rising out of a decadent and distorted one by some suddenly discovered new wonder drug called honesty and intellectual integrity has to somehow be made believable. Apart from fiddling the figures to try and demonstrate that a new day of equality and justice is just beginning to dawn a concerted effort must be made to not only change the meaning of words but to control their use. Therefore, in decadent democracies the state sponsored inquisition has a list of prescribed words, phrases, books, ideas and concepts that are considered so dangerous that it becomes a crime to even suggest that they should be accessed.

This limitation of speech and thought is naturally a prerequisite for upholding their new, modern, revised and authorised meaning of the phrase 'free speech'. Any individual is now free to say what the state states that they are allowed to say. The inquisition however is totally free to publicly abuse those peoples and cultures that they do not yet control but those so abused are not free to speak in return. If the inquisition is free to abuse people, then people in return must be free to abuse the inquisition in any manner they see fit. But dysfunctional democracies and their sick societies cannot see it that way because they do not have any concept of cultural reciprocity. They rely totally upon political rectification whereby to ensure that the 'us and them' foundationalist thinking of their dictatorships is kept constant, figures are manipulated, the meaning of words changed or deliberately misunderstood and a smoke screen of the enemies' past crimes is raised in order to allow themselves to be seen as the good guys by adjusting the scales of reality to point downwards to those bad guys who naturally not having heard of modernism live in the bad old days before democracy spread its angelic wings to protect the poor and dispossessed.

The need for a constant adjustment to make the home side look favourable requires a constant adjustment to the meaning of words and thus the meaning of language. Accordingly political rectification can be subdivided into polit-ical correctness and political correction and political propaganda. Political correctness simply means saying what you are told to say, and political correc-tion simply means the results of not saying what you are told to say.

Unstable, unjust and perverted political systems are by their very nature unbalanced and unstable and thus require a whole array of defence mecha-nisms to fool the foolish and deflect those mortal wounds caused by honesty, openness and justice.

But man has been designed to understand messages and all universal messages concerning what is right, fair and proper and fitting for mankind are simple to understand and are clearly demonstrable by simply observing the results of not following their straightforward advice.

Needless to say, the simple messages that nature gives us and that stable and coherent cultures adhere to, are not to everybody's liking. Why? Because just as the mind controls the body, the mind itself is controllable and controlled by those objective and universal truths that define the proper role and purpose of man's awareness of himself relative to nature and his fellow creatures.

But since the beginning of time there has been a festering hatred of those universal objective truths because being objective, that is not defined by any particular mind and thus the product of all well balanced and rational healthy minds, they represent the sum of man's intellectual abilities to form just and fair societies based upon those principles that his intellect has discovered to be essential and which time has proved to be indispensable and that need to be enshrined in a system of universal governance that controls all aspects of an individual's life including the manner in which he is governed and the political systems that should be adopted to enforce the dictates of that culture.

Thus, without overseeing and overriding cultural safeguards democracies, if they are the adopted political system, can easily become degenerate and if those degenerate democracies destroy those hereditary cultural safeguards that dictated what was of value, then without any cultural criterion of correctness decadent democracies degenerate even further and become decadent dictatorial democracies.

Unfortunately, decadent dictatorial democracies then set about dictating to its people what their culture is to be, that is, their culture is prescribed for them thus their culture becomes a sectarian based individualistic culture based upon the dictates of the state. But the state does not possess the objective authority of their original culture, if they ever had one, accordingly they become bitterly aware of the tentative nature of their edicts, so much so that they are forced to use overbearing and heavy-handed tactics to enforce their will.

The result is a sectarian based dogmatic culture that upholds the values of those divisive and elitist principles that formed the basis of its political ideology. One ends up with a degenerate dictatorial dogmatic democracy which enforces sectarian bigotry as a means to destabilise its electorate and to terrorise them into being submissive drones whose daily lives are controlled by a state sponsored inquisition.

The few remaining civilised societies to be found upon this planet are thus required to try and act as moderators to those extremes to be found in those societies who base their social systems upon sectarian materialistic bigotry, whose cultures are founded upon divisions, and who accrue to themselves a disproportionate amount of power and wealth which enables them to abuse and misuse others in their unending quest for superiority.

But to remain superior to everyone else takes a lot of effort and a lot of hot air to keep their balloon sized lies floating around in the stratosphere out of reach and out of sight. To lie means to place an idea or object outside and beyond the reach of another. If another rational and intellectually competent being cannot get hold of the idea and thus analyse it and judge its value and worth, then that idea lies outside the domain of human consciousness and awareness and if it lies outside a particular person, it is a particular lie and if it lies outside all people's then it is a universal lie.

Decadent democracies delight in telling universal lies and decadent democracies delight in deception. The two major methods of state deception are to claim that what they would like to talk about and discuss with their citizens is so secret that if anyone heard it they would instantly die from shock and the other method is to put all their arguments and reasons for their last act of obscenity into a drum and rotate it so fast that the major issues involved blur into a meaningless mass.

Decadent democracies have found this so useful that all forms of news are now high-speed renditions of chopped up, pre-digested, digitally modified glimpses of reality with all the pips and other nasty bits removed.

This behaviour has led to a type of intellectual terrorism which believes that all that information that might be of use and value to others must be degraded and trivialised by delivering that information in short bursts of disconnected and fragmentary slices mixed in with a barrage of irrelevant statistics and non-relevant juicy gossip.

9 Intellectual/Cultural Terrorism

IF A MAN can be sentenced to death or lifelong restraint by a jury, then what does it take to condemn a nation to a lifetime of misery? Greed! and everyone wanting a slice of the communal cake to be in direct proportion to their self-appointed importance. It may be noted however that a jury is a more or less random selection of people who unlike politicians are not subjected to those pressures to perform and conform to party political propaganda that requires them to abuse and pervert their own consciences in order to acquiesce to those manipulations of truth thought necessary to rectify a public image that might otherwise show them to be tainted and tarnished.

Furthermore, having no personal interest in the outcome of any trial they are free to follow their consciences and are equally free from any preconceptions as to what they may or may not decide. Another benefit of the random selection of decision makers is that they are unhackneyed and unmoved by the duty that befalls them for their reign is short and spares them the relentless pounding of those interested parties ever wishing to pervert the course of justice towards themselves. Being in the main down to earth they are usually above those finer forms of flattery bestowed upon them by those who would advocate that they should abandon their natural born intelligence and replace it with a more modern version that supports a self-interested version of reality in which they are so indispensable because they must obviously know what is best for themselves and thus others or they would not have been chosen in the first place and therefore because they are chosen people they therefore should assume that they are somehow superior.

To safeguard against vested interests juries are directed to have their intellect act upon the evidence alone. Thus if the accused enters the dock wearing a yellow jumper with a black hooped pattern carrying a bag marked 'swag' with a silver candlestick protruding and on being asked to remove his mask and the handkerchief from his face before giving plea to which he said 'cor blimey guv, it's a fair cop' then unless one lived in a sick society with a perverse culture that was continually stupefied and mesmerised by lies, cheating and general filth then the culprit would almost certainly be convicted and made to suffer what penalty society decides.

Naturally in degenerate cultures in which everything is a numerical relationship between reality and what the marvels of modern science tell us is possible then as everything is now theoretically possible then with us having lived so long in cartoon land it becomes a distinct possibility. Thus it 'was' theoretically possible that this particular felon 'was' going to a fancy dress party that 'might' possibly have been cancelled because everyone had died of bird flu because one of the guests had turned up as a chicken and yes the culprit could have left his lighter at home and found a discarded candlestick with a half used candle that was inadvertently dropped by a partially blind duchess on the way to a church bazaar. Yes, it is theoretically possible, but is it likely?

How then do theoretical numerical possibilities become real? Well ask your leaders and the political systems they hide behind and that they adopt to run reality!

If decadent democracies insist on utilising hordes of self-interested parasitic organisms which attach themselves to that party whose perversions are most likely to be adopted by a mesmerised and dysfunctional electorate and who are not only predisposed to cheat and lie to support their allegiances but are predetermined to distort their own honour and their rationality in order to maintain the numerical superiority of their intellectually senile allies then how can such organisations truly reflect the wishes of the electorate?

The intellect granted to man by nature is solely concerned with what is called transcendental philosophy. One cannot go around picking up objects and shoving them through the eye sockets or poking them up the nose so that the mind can have a good look at them. Their physicality must first be converted into electrodynamic forces which transcend the objectivity of nature. Once the essentials of any object are transformed into sensory perception a process known as geometric conversion places these perceptions before the mind which decodes the information and presents this information in the form of ideas before the intellect. But the intellect just sees a jumble of messages and bits and pieces of a puzzle and a load of dots and dashes. It doesn't have a clue as to what they are or what they signify for without some form of guidelines as to how to reconstruct the evidence then it will lie around uselessly rotting away in insignificance. To use an analogy in which the intellect is the piano whilst the body, the senses etc. are its component parts then those ideas in the form of dots and dashes are the music, which are derived from nature and the environment. Culture becomes the composer and the music teacher.

It is one's culture that decides what significance and importance is to be attached to that which comes before the intellect. It is culture that composes the picture of reality. Different cultures compose different tunes and melodies which they teach using different techniques. However, no matter the different and differing types and styles of music they all have one purpose and no matter how big or small or what colour or how constructed all pianos are designed to interpret that music in a style acceptable to the cultural expectations of the audience, i.e. society. If a pianist was to play a recent composition to reflect that diversity to be found in divisive and culturally fragmented societies then they would be forced to play discordant and inharmonious music and if the audience tried to leave the management would be forced to lock the doors.

Clearly if expectations are to be cruelly disappointed and reality distorted to fit the desires of the decadent then large numbers of dysfunctional pianists are required to proclaim that the old-style music is obsolete and that they themselves are to take over complete control of what is written, how it is performed and what the whole meaningless discordant mess means. Anyone who does not daily subscribe to this united one world interpretation, or does not think it fit or proper, is therefore classified as a dissident to dissonance and must be eliminated. To ignore the wishes of others is natural, to ignore the rationality of man is normal but to ignore the intellectual arguments of men who wish for peace and harmony is a crime against humanity.

To allow the collective intelligence of this world to be insulted by those perverted pianists who squander vast resources upon synthesising reality into a disjointed and divisive form of discordant music which extols the virtues of dishonesty and is heard echoing aloud in that perpetual hell that is reserved for such wickedness, makes one a cultural coward. Cultural cowards sing along with the rest of them hoping not to be noticed, not to be singled out, not to be fingered and to be cast out of the darkness and into the electric arc lamps of the new inquisition and their rabid bloodhounds in the media.

True men do not fear the distorted dribblings of the demented. They speak out no matter the cost. Sick societies and cultures however never wish to know how sick they really are – after all they have squandered the world's resources on attempting to cure the incurable. That natural hate and a quest for vengeance that arises when their faults are found does not direct itself at the causes but only those who suggest them. Accordingly, those that have the intellectual freedom to not only suggest the causes but also the cure must be silenced.

Those cultural and intellectual freedoms that naturally arise when men are free – free to create their own worlds in which they hunt for food, build their own houses, brew beer, grow crops and procreate, and create cultures and societies in which each and every member is of equal worth, and all these things without the help or interference from politicians, social workers, estate agents, profit mongers, scientists and other non-productive polluters, are dancing to their own tunes. But these melodic airs drive the dictators of democratic disorder demented. They cannot rest, they pace up and down hatching plots of vicious reprisal because they are unable to control the laughter and enjoyment that is given free by nature. This leads to a permanent war in which like all other wars the first casualty is truth itself. Next the propaganda machine founded upon the ruins of truth and decency sends out its inquisitors to re-educate the uneducated in the new state sponsored and directed meaning of words. They then make public pronouncements that not only are numbers to be the intellectual copyright of the decadent, but the genetic copyright of every living individual is state property. To deny either is a crime punishable by disappearance.

Food is genetic material and thus can be fiddled with. Shelter in all forms must be obtained through a lifetime of slavery or rented at exorbitant or at an obscene cost to the dispossessed unless living in the wastelands of state sponsored slums. Warmth is to be achieved by ensuring that any nation that is built upon almost unlimited supplies of naturally combustible materials should have such wealth so mismanaged in its production and utilisation that it becomes unavailable to the poor.

No legitimate questions concerning the abuses by pornocracies are now permitted, for those rulers who prostitute their ethical and moral values for a handful of gold and a bunch of dilapidated dwellings are only fit to shovel shit from one ship to another.

It is a cultural and moral duty incumbent upon men who have the necessary intellectual capacity and integrity to defeat these miserable squirts and to replace their outdated and elitist perversions with strong and equitable cultures.

It is therefore the job of these miserable squirts to ensure their survival by the imposition of draconian rules and regulations upon their subjects in order to silence their natural born enemies. It is the imposition of such unjust laws such as these that condemn the majority of the world to suffer unnecessary hardship and suffering.

If these rules and regulations are left unchallenged then who can be considered innocent? If full and open debates are not permitted so that the real causes of those injustices that plague the world are held up to the light of reason, then ordinary people will be forced to take extreme measures to highlight those moral and ethical injustices that are being hidden behind the mesh of modernism which declares that decency is dead.

10 Fragmentation and Division

IT IS DIFFICULT not to repeat time and again the dangers to humanity posed by all those diseased and culturally dysfunctional political parasites that are endemic to decadent democracies. Their main delight is to enforce their divisive dogmas in order that the poor and dispossessed remain so whilst new legislation is enacted by their cronies and lapdogs by which the rich and greedy can widen the economic gap between them and their inferiors which enables them to afford the luxury of buying up yet more noisome rot boxes and become the common man's dream of becoming a slum landlord.

To avoid any disruption to the economic nightmare that becomes necessary to support such profligacy the true men of such societies must either be subverted by the tyranny of depravity and greed or emasculated by the handing over of all natural born rights, privileges and freedoms that they enjoy; these to be divided amongst corrupt politicians, their supporters and the now obligatory quota of malignant hags who act as their groupies.

Any act to regain natural born freedoms and a life of human dignity out of the control and reach of the parasitic are construed as acts of terror.

The one world order as ordered by western decadent democracies state that all nations must bow down to this new world order. Any nation that objected would invite the illegitimate and indiscriminate use of vast amounts of firepower to destroy the innocent, their homes and their livelihoods and the population as a whole subjected to random acts of mindless violence.

Great cultures arise by asking nature what it wants in return for it providing man with the essentials of life. It has taken nature countless eons to defragment creation and to heal the planet by locking away those poisons and pollutants that would make life upon its surface unbearable and intolerable. It has asked us not to indulge ourselves at its expense by allowing that original sin of greed and thirst for that which is not ours to destroy the delicate balance that has taken so long to achieve.

It therefore has granted man a supreme awareness in order that he may act as a guardian and has granted him that intellectual ability to understand that to preserve the balance between good and evil he must create cultures that treat every creature upon its surface as of equal worth.

This equal worth arises because every single created organism has its own special role within that order of life that has taken so long to perfect. However the value to this planet of each living organism is judged when its individual actions are made relative to its naturally assigned role and these are then held up against and made relative to those codes of conduct that form the criteria of correctness, (that is that correct behaviour and conduct) that demonstrates the objective ideals of a culture as to whether or not the individual is acting in a proper and suitable manner.

If not, then it becomes a diseased organism for it unsettles that balance within life that must necessarily exist so that other organisms may live at ease. It is the job of diseased organisms to make all other organisms ill at ease by disturbing nature through a vicious and unwarranted interference and by employing mindless henchmen to unlock those poisons and pollutants and to spread them throughout the globe.

This abuse of man's creativity not only endangers the seeds of life themselves but distorts and destroys those cultures founded upon the need to educate and guide others as to how best to show respect to others and how to honour what nature provides us free of charge.

The aim of cultural education is to turn all those creatures who would otherwise blindly follow the path that greed has made so inviting and that jealousy has taken great pains in guarding, into well balanced individuals capable of using their different talents and capabilities to enrich this planet by repaying some of the outstanding debt which we owe it.

However cultural education must be carefully selective so that it caters for the needs of those which nature has chosen to create strong and creative cultures.

To stifle an individual talent for running or gymnastics by a moronic attempt to bunch everyone together into one lump in a cost cutting exercise to teach everyone the same subjects at the same time is as mindless as destroying an individual's intellectual interests by forcing them to learn mathematics and chemistry to which they may not be suited and have absolutely no aptitude.

But in sick societies it is more or less obligatory to lump the masses together in some form of comprehensive cultural prison in order that they never learn what it is to be a human being and how to think correctly for if this were to occur our offspring would quickly understand the grotesque deformity of their cultural bankruptcy.

In education as in life what is fit and proper for one child may not be fit and proper for another. Furthermore, what is fit and proper for males is rarely fit and proper for females, for nature has assigned them different tasks and therefore differing rates of development. Nature does this in an attempt to protect itself from the consequences of those abominations that arise when interfering busybodies usurp justice and fairness by enforcing others to conform to their ideas of how people should develop irrespective of their physical or mental capabilities, in order that the resultant human becomes fit for either factory fodder or is able to attach themselves to an elitist regime by proving how hungry they have become to be regarded as superior by having been force fed that misinformed information necessary to deny reality and to pervert conscious justice.

This newly developed clone that espouses the usual propaganda of perversion believes themselves to be a superior being who is thus more deserving, more important and more everything, this false pride leading to a type of individualism that views other beings as somehow inferior and thus to be used and abused to finance those excesses that greedy clones have been educated to expect. Once pride and greed take possession of the intellect then the individual is incapable of self-control for greed, and pride have no natural boundaries or enemies other than cultural ones. But if the culture of a nation has been destroyed and debased by a numerical interpretation of value and worth and has then been replaced by a popular culture based upon greed and avarice then as no cultural safeguards exist humpty dumpty will get fatter and fatter until his head is so large they will have to enlarge the doors of his mansions and rented slums so that he can politely enquire as to how well the oppressed are coping with their oppression.

Unfortunately, when pride and greed are married to power then all life is at risk. Those unfortunate creatures who live under the tyrannical rule of the popular cultures of greed, interference, violence and pride of possessions are thus forced to spend the days of their lives in a slavish attempt to perfect themselves in order that they may be seen to conform to the new ideals of that health and happiness that must follow from becoming a modern man or woman.

Accordingly in the polished plastic and chrome culture of modernism vast sums must be squandered to polish people to an unnatural degree of perfection so that nature itself and the order it has granted us may be derided as out of date old fashioned nonsense. Those naturally arising standards of decent behaviour that have been imposed so that the normal diseases and deformities necessary to keep mankind in check are not subjected to a dishonourable attack by those greedy profit managers who are ever keen to profit from another's misfortunes are cast aside for it can now be statistically proven that if you look good you must feel good irrespective of the spiritual and mental damage that might be reeked upon those who embark upon such an illusory path to perfection.

The visual arts in such popular cultures must therefore concentrate upon the predicted results of that polished perfection so that as medical science has advanced by such a wonderful degree and diseases and imperfections are almost a thing of the past, they feel entitled to display countless air brushed images of silicone enhanced perfection at all and every opportunity.

But nature only provides imperfections in order to remind us that they are essential to keep us from straying too far from that which binds us all together, that tenuous human frailty that keeps all humanity in one great cultural chain of being and bound together by a respect for each other and the environment.

If we were all perfect then we would be angels, but angels cannot do what we have to do for they are fixed, constant and timeless entities. We are inconstant, mobile, time related creatures who are given simple and easily understood tasks to perform and simple rules to follow, yet that malignancy that inevitably arises in others who become disgruntled and disaffected by their share of and in existence has now grown to such an extent that they have perverted truth and reality for their own selfish ends.

A naturally arising intellectual principle known as the 'principle of sufficient reasoning' states that any natural object possesses only that which is necessary for that object to function the way it was designed to and possesses only that which is necessary for it to successfully fulfil that function. Thus, each individual is allotted a fixed and more or less constant degree of those physical and intellectual capabilities thought necessary to fulfil their natural role and thus to demand or to take more than one's allotted share is simply a form of greed. Accordingly, all coherent and civilised cultures recognise that each and every existent individualised naturally occurring object is given all that it needs to perform whatever task it has been created to accomplish.

A little thought may demonstrate the inevitability of this life appearing from an individualistic viewpoint as sometimes grossly unfair, but it is only unfair from a particular viewpoint which judges such matters with such a degree of self-interest and fear that it can have no wider cultural application. If a creature dies deformed at birth, then it has served its purpose. As a minute part of a whole existent universe, we cannot know how this event relates to the whole of creation, but we can assure ourselves it is not meaningless.

It is of no relevance if nearly all creatures are thus destined to die, for as minute parts of the whole we cannot comprehend nor encompass that whole nor should we attempt to for it is wrong because it is futile and it wastes away our allotted time upon improper pursuits. Our individual task is rarely to keep looking over the fence and poking our noses into other people's affairs. The first job of all sentient human beings is to educate themselves to a degree of intellectual capability that will enable them to decipher those not well overly concealed clues as to their particular purpose within their life and thus within their society and their culture.

It is the job of all self-interested parasitic, interfering, self-appointed busybodies to not only prevent others from discovering the truth to their own realities but to possess and hide all those naturally occurring clues and if possible, hold a society and its culture to ransom by promising to deliver them without actually doing so. This form of political blackmail is essential to all decadent democracies.

It is the job of true men to create strong and coherent cultures that possess the necessary intellectual and moral authority to demonstrate the absurdity of those that choose a path that leads to a determined effort to destroy all naturally arising values of justice and fairness and to replace them with a vicious campaign of jealous hatred against whoever or whatever created this universe.

The cultures of death and destruction, of possession and dispossession that accompany these diseased organisms cast the living world into a despondency that no amount of prayer or pleading can terminate.

These diseased organisms depend upon the numerical sciences to deflect and defuse all legitimate intellectual arguments as to the validity of their regimes. In order to justify the unjustifiable, corrupt regimes adopt a self-justifying non-flexible system of accountability that employs numbers to interpret reality.

This is considered indispensable because numbers can be readily altered, moved and fiddled with so no matter how inaccurate they become in reflecting reality the producers of such meaningless symbolic representations of truth can simply state that that is what they meant to say and justify this statement by referring to another set of self-referential numbers and so on. As one set of numbers can always be made to refer to another set of numbers then reality becomes an abstract concept and thus reality can be made to conform to the numerical evidence and not the other way round.

One of the consequences therefore of living in a sick society with a decadent and perverted democratic system and a popular culture based upon self-satisfying principles is that everything must be given a numerical value even though in itself it may be worthless.

Accordingly, the polished people of modernism attempt to conform to the purveyors of pleasure and misinformation who persistently confuse and confound quantity with quality. This is a deliberate act of perversion so that others inherit a culturally perverted obsession with themselves in which the physical and intellectual self are separated and then recombined into one single unit which then permits the self to enter into an unending and ultimately futile quest to alter the physicality of the whole into a shape and order that accords with those numerical dimensions that arise when size becomes synonymous with success and quantity becomes synonymous with pleasure.

Those qualities that make life worthwhile and give it a natural reality are thus consigned to that tip heap that contains the remains of all those that have fought throughout time to uphold decency, honour and intellectual integrity that are the hallmark of all true men. But the riff-raff and scum perverted by greed and a jealousy of others who hold their vile usury in the contempt it deserves are driven by a hatred arising out of their awareness of their own intellectual deficiencies and so they wish to make sure that if they are to go down the slide of selfishness into oblivion, misery and perpetual self-recrimination then they will drag as many innocent bystanders as they can down with them. Thus they enjoy a perverse delight in spoiling the story with revealing the ending and with changing the plot so that it reflects their fetish for politically correct statistical representation of numerically disadvantaged minorities as being of value to a story the point of which is that each and every individual is given carte blanche to interpret in their own way and to interpret the meaning as they see fit themselves.

But these interfering do-gooders do harm. There is not just one story, one history, one world. One cannot go around shoving garbage and gobbledegook down the throats of people from a few months old so when it is regurgitated with the cold cow's milk mother's milk substitute the delighted onlookers can marvel at their own ability to intellectually traumatise their offspring before they have even learnt to walk.

The job of true men is to create a culture in which everyone has the time, space, love and attention to discover this planet for themselves without some self-righteous, hypocritical, sectarian bigot ramming politically motivated mindless statistical drivel down their throats.

But mindless statistical drivel when combined with mindlessly complex descriptive definitions of what is lawful, legal and legitimate so empower the parasitic that only strong and legitimate cultures can destroy these pests. What they say is the law is not always legal and rarely legitimate for the law means how matters lie in reality. But as stated reality is totally dependent upon how things are presented to us. It does not reside in the objects themselves. Precisely. If the law resided in the object itself and the object itself was a culturally legitimate object, then that object would be a legal representation of reality.

Accordingly if the object is a person – a human being with a personal identity specific to themselves and thus a completely individuated being and if the single living unit is granted absolute rights then that individual becomes the law in so far as they represent the reality of their own situation and not as it is at present where the law resides with those debauched deformities who inhabit a world of embezzlement and misappropriation who are ever ready to prostitute themselves by soliciting customers who wish to emulate their peers by becoming the willing victims of naturally occurring circumstance.

So where exactly does the law reside? Well, it naturally resides in each and every one of us. In practice it resides in that malignancy of power known as statute law. But statute laws are synthetic structures, they are devised by debauched deviants to further their own perverted ends and like all statues that stand for a while they meet that inevitable fate that awaits all that is unveiled in that pomp and circumstance that surrounds morally and ethically and intellectually inferior beings.

It requires no lawyers, solicitors or any officers of law to judge whether or not an absolute right of an individual being is being transgressed because in strong coherent cultures the laws are not only self-evident they self-evidently reside in the person themselves and if the person themselves goes to a tribunal of their fellow members it will be self-evident if an offence to the cultural integrity of their society has occurred. The foundation for an individual bill of rights must therefore depend upon universal principles of fairness and justice which however are complete strangers to the one world mind fix of decadent western democracies.

It is the job of true men who have that natural inborn intellectual capacity unperverted by greed and avarice to restore the natural balance and order of life for without true men corrupt political systems will permit and encourage human depravity to bring every existent creature down to a meaningless level of existence in order to convert them into mindless polling station fodder.

True men must learn to ignore all such abominations. They must also ignore those hormonally challenged malignant hags who are proud to have become those grotesque deformities of womanhood who have been empowered to inflict their hideously malformed ideas as to what constitutes a just and fair society upon the innocent and disinterested. These intellectually subnormal manifestations of emotional instability are at the forefront of destroying and devaluing worthwhile cultural values in a perverse attempt to justify their own seedy actions.

But just as true men understand that they have an inborn duty to create strong and coherent cultures using their intellectual creativity then true women also understand that they have an inborn duty to nurture that culture using their physical creativity so as to enable that culture to grow and remain strong and vigorous.

11 Culture

WHAT IS CULTURE? Culture means to cultivate and to nurture. It is the eurhythmic harmonious functioning between the active and the passive, the virile and the fertile. Well balanced cultures are therefore good cultures. A coherent culture is one in which its members stick together for the sake of their society as a whole. This coherence of purpose manifests itself throughout every facet of life. It is reflected in the faces of its peoples, in their streets and houses, in their homes and in their workplaces. It is visible in their pastimes and in the books and magazines they read, in the programmes and films that they watch.

A strong, healthy and equitable culture is denoted by its openness and if the culture is well balanced and harmonious there will be an atmosphere of contentment brought about by living in an environment which is both stable and constant. This constancy of cohesion permits a nation with a strong cultural heritage to display their gratitude for what nature has given them, and they are thus disposed to express goodwill to their fellow creatures. Accordingly, when people are content and satisfied with their lot, they display a marked degree of civility and politeness that amounts to a genuine affection towards other cultures, and they thus tolerate all others to live in that peace and tranquillity that they possess themselves.

Culture therefore becomes that essential criteria through and by which the essential characteristics of humankind and their nature are categorised into their proper order of importance to maintaining a just and equitable social system. This enables members of such cultures to formulate codes of conduct that are suitable for each member according to their role within that society and which leads to the establishment of what society considers fitting and proper for that member to undertake and attempt relative to those criteria of correctness that stipulates that the whole is always greater than the part. This principle ensures that particular examples of injustices and individual disagreements do not and cannot become generalised and then universalised to the detriment of the whole as is endemic in dysfunctional decadent democracies with sick societies and deformed cultures. Thus, western popular cultures and broadcasting systems become a voyeuristical dreamland of never-ending divisionary disputes concerning particular examples of stupidity which are somehow touted as representing a general trend within their sick society which is further universalised in order to bring all existent individuals down to their own perverted level of intellectual incompetence.

In strong and viable cultures all laws inhere in the subject, that is, it is the individual person who represents those laws necessary to uphold human dignity. Thus, every individual in an intellectually competent culture represents, in themselves, those values that are necessary to uphold the honour and dignity of every living creature. Laws, rules and regulations imposed upon them by perverted political regimes therefore have no cultural and thus no moral value or validity. Each individual who attaches themselves to a particular culture and who agrees to be bound by those cultural contracts necessary to ensure fair play is therefore empowered by that culture and protected by that culture. They should therefore be safe from the fads of fashion and the mindless interference that naturally arise when precarious political systems wish to enforce their own popular perversions of reality upon the disinterested. But parasitic, perverted, political abominations delight in enforcing their belief systems upon others for they employ a kind of mindless interference and bullying that renders every human action a source of revenue as well as a source for concerned busybodies to meddle with.

Cultures are those objectively, justifiable human constructs that are the embodiment of those values that humans have throughout time and through time have come to regard as essential in allowing every living creature to fulfil their purpose in a proper and suitable manner.

If cultures are allowed to function without political and social interference then those endowed by nature with the necessary intellectual awareness and capacity will be left free to formulate cultural laws that will form the basis for those cultural contracts necessary for civilised living and which will also legitimise and validate the actions of those who agree to be bound by such contracts and who thus feel obliged to protect and honour their culture when it is subjected to the unwanted attentions that arise when the jealousy of greed and the hatred of living in a self-inflicted cultural inferiority is compounded with the emotional instability and intellectual incompetence to be found in sick and perverted societies.

Intellectually competent cultures that possess clear, simple and readily understood laws enshrined within their works of art and within their social structures become civilised societies that can progress to civilisations which on intellectual, ethical, moral and rational grounds are above those weapons used by all degenerates that wish to challenge the proper order of civilised life.

Great cultures therefore ignore numerical interpretations of worth and value. Every living organism is accorded its rightful place within the great ordering of life.

Great cultures despise the parasitic practices of the usurer. Culture makes the real world go round. Money simply makes the millstones of misery revolve remorselessly as they grind people down.

Great cultures allow their followers healthy and legitimate expressions of their creativity and thus despise the pornographers who wish ever to debase humanity by making the mind a slave to greed and the body a prisoner of depravity.

All intellectually coherent cultures reject politically motivated assertions that imply that one culture can because one is more numerically powerful than another be superior to another by it being numerically more powerful.

All great cultures would recognise the uniqueness of each of its members and would treat them as of being equally indispensable. To this end the laws of such societies would be inalienable, that is, would reside in every living creature born into that society. They would therefore not be external or abstract and thus outside the jurisdiction and control of those universal principles that are necessary to safeguard great civilisations from degenerating into perverted, political, popular cultures with self-greed and self-aggrandizement as their main priority.

Accordingly, all laws would be universal cultural laws which were represented by and through and be inherent in each and every creature that was bound by the culture of their nation.

Those laws used to justify those transient political expedients that underpin the perverted practices of politicians and their henchmen and supporters would therefore have no cultural validity. Degenerate democracies which used numerical interpretations of popularity and the numerical superiority of intellectually subnormal lapdogs in their legislature to force through divisive and demeaning laws to further subjugate their dysfunctional electorate into a meaningless life of drudgery could possess no influence or legitimacy to alter the fundamental cultural rights that are inherent in the lives of all true men.

It is true men who transcend life. It is true men who create great cultures, and it is morally deformed political maggots who destroy them.

True men creating great cultures, would not require the legitimacy of such cultures to be dependent upon power or wealth. Culture and political parties are both intellectual abstractions. But whereas political parties will always be intellectual abstractions and therefore non-essential and thus disposable, culture uses art to objectify those ideals that arise when people vote for a just and fair universal society founded upon a proportionate distribution of the commonwealth to be found upon this planet and that belongs, as of right, to every creature that moves upon its surface.

No government, no law, no religion, no god, no party, no weapon, no idea, no thing can alter this concept nor deny it. It is however under constant attack by those vicious, greedy, evil thugs who use terror and violence to upset and destroy all decent and honourable cultural values, and it is only cultural cowardice that allows such perversions to persist. Accordingly cultural cowards and the societies to which they belong can never consider themselves to be innocent and must therefore share the harm and distress caused by their mindless political dictators as they drag their malformed and degenerate political systems over the face of this planet in a never-ending quest to enslave others in their culturally dead and morally diseased democracies.

Great cultures bind their members together with abstract yet tangible links of honour and respect. This honour and respect leads to a cohesive society that is further enriched and enhanced by that safety and surety that a cultural constancy of purpose can alone ensure. Cultural contracts form the basis of this constancy, for once entered into they are binding and cannot be cast aside. They are like all great and meaningful concepts binding in honour only for in great cultures it is understood that to lose one's honour makes a person open to ridicule and contempt and generally unfit to be trusted. Thus, in one culture such impediments are seen as damning yet in sick ones they appear essential attributes. Accordingly, a good guide to the health of one's culture is the degree of importance that that culture attaches to those contracts between its members which since time began have been thought necessary for a productive and worthwhile existence.

12 Cultural Contracts

IT IS THE cultural contracts of a nation which empower the laws of that nation. It is the cultural contracts of a nation which legitimises the political systems of a nation. Cultural contracts are absolutely necessary for maintaining human dignity and human dignity is dependent upon all living creatures being considered to be of equal worth in linking life together in a rational, fair and meaningful form.

Cultural contracts form the universal laws that are independent of man and independent of time. They are the objective criteria by and through which all life is measured. They are absolute intellectual constructs and thus cannot have conditions imposed upon them by any particular society or culture. They are objective realities that are not produced by any particular individual or nation for they are those concepts that all minds free from self-interested greed and pride would consider to be just and fair.

The cultural contracts of a nation are therefore those absolute objective criteria by which societies and their adopted political systems are to be judged. Particular societies and their political systems are therefore transient non-essential human constructs that are subordinate to those universal cultural values that form the reason and justification of those cultural contracts that form the basis of civilised societies.

The universal cultural values to which all free civilised societies would consider reasonable, proper, fair and just and to which they should perpetually refer to when forming their essential cultural contracts to order their daily lives and relationships exist in a timeless, intellectual and spiritual sanctuary that is independent to existence itself for all or any creator would have to formulate them and be guided by them before any materialisation of those creatures required to enact and fulfil their purpose and thus give them credibility could be started. Thus, in the beginning are the words, the concepts and the ideas and these must precede life itself and thus are independent of life itself.

These universal intellectual constructs form the basis of all religions and therefore all religions owe their allegiances towards them. Accordingly, all religions are equal before and in front of these contracts and therefore no religion can claim precedence or superiority over another.

Religions as well as political systems are subordinate to universal codes of values and the human contracts entered into using particular cultural constructs to validate and justify how people wish to lead their lives.

As the universal codes of conduct which are based upon the values that underpin civilised humanity form the intellectual and rational validity for those rules and regulations that control and direct the relationships between living creatures are the basis of all just laws then any law that is dishonourable, that is, one that is enacted through political motives to alter the naturally occurring relationships between living creatures based upon economic, social and financial or political expediency are culturally and morally invalid. As all manmade laws are abstract constructs, if those forming those laws belong to a culture that time has demonstrated to be a dishonourable one by the failure of successive generations of its leaders and their minions to honour their treaties and pledges and who have been shown to act in a selfish and belligerent manner then such a culture is a dishonourable one and thus its laws whether common or statute can be flouted at will for all and every law requires men of honour not only to formulate and enact them but to honour and respect them.

All cultural contracts depend upon the honour of those that enter into them, and they depend upon the honour of a nation's people as a whole.

A whole nation can therefore act dishonourably as each individual is responsible for the actions of their elected representatives.

An honourable person therefore is one who takes an individual responsibility to educate themselves into a position whereby they are able to understand what a necessary truth is and what is mere political or economic drivel. They have a responsibility to themselves and their culture to conduct themselves in a manner that will not bring disgrace or dishonour to their fellow creatures.

They have an intellectual duty to ensure that that rational space of awareness that the mind generates in order that it may think clearly is kept as free as possible from those false and distorted images that are the trademarks of the profit mongers and the perverted.

What therefore can an individual do to ensure that what is shown in that private cinema inside their head is suitable?

Fortunately, this is not an individual responsibility, it is a collective cultural one. The purpose of correct cultures is to filter out falsehoods and to prohibit the perversions of the profit mongers.

Censorship means to take into account. Censorship means to hold to account. Cultural censorship therefore means to take into account on behalf of the humanity of a nation as a whole the effect that falsehood, distortion and perversions will have upon and in the minds of those who look to their cultural heritage to protect them and safeguard them from those who prey upon and mercilessly interfere with others.

Cultural censorship is therefore absolutely necessary for it not only takes into account the intellectual and thus spiritual harm that certain falsehoods will do to immature and fragile minds, but it will also hold those who trade in such perversions for profit to account.

Societies that are permitted to mature in that climate of constancy that cultural censorship makes possible, become intellectually and spiritually stable civilisations. The stable culture and religions of such civilisations form the basis of what is taught to the young and what is used to guide the old in their decision making. The young are thus permitted to reach a degree of understanding and maturity whereby the falsehoods of greed and the jealousy of the perverse can be seen for what they are.

A culture thus enriched by such people will always be spiritually rich thus has no need for economic or numerical supremacy.

A culturally rich nation understands that a simple act of kindness or forgiveness enriches their human dignity whereas every act of greed and avarice debases humanity and places an unbearable and disproportionate burden upon other living creatures and upon the planet itself.

For the words of creation to have meaning requires people to enact their purpose. For cultural contracts to have validity it requires those who enter into them to have been educated by their culture to a degree that makes them capable of understanding the commitments necessary for their society to function correctly.

If such competence cannot be demonstrated, then different degrees of contract would be necessary. But human nature cannot and does not alter for it has been formulated and set out before humans evolved. Thus, people will always be tempted to cheat and lie to further their own ends, yet even if they enter into a cultural contract with perverted intentions then that contract and the commitments entered into must be honoured.

There is a never ending supply of vile practitioners who are ever keen to prostitute themselves and their honour through soliciting trade from those who are unaware that they have been unjustly empowered by malformed, divisive and thus obscene laws which were enacted by intellectually and morally subnormal parasitic political organisms seeking a temporary popularity with the electorate by disenfranchising free people from their cultural right to have their contracts honoured.

Great civilisations and cultures understand the concept of constancy. Great civilisations and cultures understand that a man's word is his bond. Great civilisations and cultures understand that creatures apart from true men possess no natural honour and thus possess no shame. Great civilisations and cultures therefore must not only be censorial they must also be discriminatory.

To discriminate means to note and to take into account the differences between two or more objects.

Thus to discriminate against one object merely because it is an individual representation of a particular class of objects would be irrational and therefore wrong, but it can never be wrong or false to discriminate against an individual object if the differences that that object represents are such that, when made relative to a particular culture, that this individual proves to be acting without respect, without honour and with an open and clear intention to harm that particular culture to which they have been made relative to. Accordingly, one has a cultural duty to protect one's culture from harm, from whatever source.

As stated, cultural contacts, to be meaningful, require that those who freely enter into them need to be educated to understand the implications of such agreements and the personal responsibility that they alone must bear in order that their culture is not brought into that disrepute that arises when individuals negligently and selfishly use their culture as a means for individualistic self-improvement in order to gain a degree of superiority and then to use that superiority to debase and demean others.

Great cultures need time because time tells no lies. Time is independent of fashion and forms the basis of all the sciences and all the religious philosophies.

Time has been granted to the intellect so that it may discover what is, then why what is is and then why it should be.

It permits man to achieve wisdom, and it empowers men to become true men and thus entitles them to despise the wilfully ignorant, wilfully greedy, and the wilfully stupid.

Great cultures therefore require time and, in the time required for them to grow, they must be protected from that wilful want of knowing, that promiscuous ignorance that is the hallmark of perverted politicians and their mentally subnormal advocates and supporters. That particular breed of vicious scum who delight in molesting others for their own profit and glorification also delight in confusing ignorance with innocence in order to permit them to perform grotesque acts of vandalism as they assume that their wilfully self-imposed ignorance will be confused and confounded with innocence. But ignorance means to ignore knowing and is the very essence of corrupt political systems. Innocence means incapable of knowing thus incapable of knowingly doing harm.

Debased and debauched, degenerate, democratic political systems deliberately do harm. Only cultural codes of conduct can control such diseased organisations. Only cultural cowardice and cowards can let them perpetrate their parasitic practices. Cultures therefore must be lawfully permitted to remove any self-perpetuating layer of scum floating upon the surface of innocent cultures and their social structures.

However physical removal is not the answer because there is an everlasting supply of candidates ever ready to prostitute themselves for the dishonourable honour of selling their souls for a few lumps of brick and stone and some bits of silver in order to be given the freedom to interfere with themselves, their neighbours and the world in an absurd desire to improve that which requires no improving. Thus that self-approving, self-appointed layer of intellectual obscenities that consider themselves not only qualified but justified in interfering with others using temporal, hypothetical beliefs as to how society and individuals ought to function to fit in with their sycophantic reverence for the new sciences of consumerism and numbers need to be removed and re-educated and taken back to a different reformatory where they are taught proper cultural values.

It is the culture of a nation that gives it its meaning and purpose and therefore its identity. It is the culture of a nation and the contracts of honour that bind its people together. It is the culture of a country that gives its words their true and proper meaning. It is those words that make civilisation possible.

13 Anomic Scepticism

IF ONE IS educated within a culture wherein the language has become debased to the extent that words possess no definite objective meaning and thus have no cultural criteria by which their correctness can be judged then people will spend their time simply shovelling words around, without any due care or attention and thus words will mean whatever one wishes them to mean.

All decadent democracies require this to happen. This political and social abuse of language leads to a wilful disregard for the truth and everyone is left free to construct their own version of reality. This then empowers them to disregard others. This breakdown of meaning leads to large sections of such societies suffering from a type of hopelessness which leads onwards towards a meaningless and miserable existence. This anomie manifests itself as a form of anomic scepticism wherein only the self matters and thus only the absence of pain to the individual self is of any consequence.

Once a society has been culturally deadened then gross acts of aggression against others can be undertaken as such obscene acts of self-interested interference in the lives of others can be explained away using those meaningless platitudes ever on the lips of those who use the language of lying to justify the unjustifiable.

The most meaningless of platitudes is one that states, 'it was ever thus' or in other words appointed by some creator. This mythical illogical nonsense has seen kings and princes ride roughshod over the cultures of many a land. It now permits those who would aspire to rule the world some pretext that this is how it was so, so this is how it should be.

But though human nature does not and cannot alter, the nature and conduct of humans is controlled by the culture of their nation, that is, the society into which they are born and educated.

If a creature is born into a gun toting consumer mad, glutinous, interfering, loud mouthed, promiscuous, culturally decadent society then that will be the nature of the human.

If the culture of that society fails to subjugate and control its political parasites then they will eat its heart and brain and leave a sick and empty shell headed by a gun toting, interfering, loud mouthed moron.

The purpose and meaning of human nature can be expressed in many forms. It is the role of culture to express those meanings thus cultures are free to choose how to express themselves thus freedom of speech but not freedom to lie, distort or pervert.

Great cultures arise through time and are called great because of the degree to which they encapsulate those timeless universal constants that make the lives of all living creatures under its protection worthwhile, meaningful and productive.

Sick cultures are awash with wretches who are ever keen to interfere with other living creatures for their own amusement and profit.

If those living creatures are defenceless, so much the better for they can then be locked away and physically and mentally mutilated for even greater pleasure and profit.

No decent honourable living creature should wish to profit or live longer at such an expense to their humanity or should tolerate the moral dangers that such perverted practices would have by distorting their cultural integrity for justice and fairness.

It may be seen therefore that cultures become great when their capacity to grow straight and thus true remains undiminished by those social evils that arise when honour and its decent intentions die.

Being founded, nurtured and supported by those constant and unchangeable universal human values that promote the value and meaning of life and make life worth living cultures will simply shrivel up and die if their members become selfish, self-interested, self-important individuals with self-appointed, self- serving rights and privileges which are governed by self-righteous, self-propagating and self-perpetuating political systems that employ self-congratulatory systems to secularise and fragment their societies to such an extent that they become sick and dysfunctional and thus unable to form any culturally cohesive confederacy capable of challenging the parasitic and degenerate democracies that feed upon them.

No matter how much is squandered upon the health services of such societies they have become culturally incurable.

Great, just and fair cultures avoid those pornographically selfish freedoms of expression which are designed to pervert the cultural freedoms and integrity of its members for profit.

Great cultures therefore protect each of its members by assigning to them a cultural copyright that cannot be used or abused by others for any reason whatsoever.

Sick and illegitimate cultures permit their diseased followers those perverted rights and privileges that are required to interfere with and ultimately destroy the lives of others. Such filth and garbage are eager to litter this planet with their pestilential inadequacies whilst proclaiming to have the interests of their fellow creatures close to their wallets and are ever ready to regurgitate a litany of historical pulp fiction in a hysterical attempt to justify and validate their present positions of power. But these positions have been attained by maintaining a constant state of terror through the use of constant campaigns of mindless and arbitrary violence against anyone or anything beyond their control. If these control freaks were to be exposed to the light of reason, that is, the natural birthright of all living creatures then they would be seen for what they are – deformed and degenerate specimens of humankind who like all parasites shrivel up and die when removed from their victims.

Nature has wisely granted us the power to reason, the power to be aware that gradually matures into our own internal judge and jury.

To avoid detection, all corrupt political systems require secrecy to avoid them being seen for what they are and for what they do.

Our conscience our own private judge and jury are given to us so that we may lead well balanced lives.

It is granted to all creatures who possess an awareness of their own unique purpose within existence so that all creatures are capable of forming a confederacy of cultures to nurture and protect those freedoms necessary for each living creature to live a decent and proper life unsullied and unmolested by self-seeking profit mongers and perverted political practitioners.

It is the individual's unique purpose within existence that proves to be a mortal danger to the one world theorists for such ideas destroy the concept of the monoculture wherein we become perfectly polished clones neatly packaged to fit the popular cultures of the perverted parasites.

The ultimate aim of a cultural philosophy is to discover a logical and rational framework by and through which the intellect can construct meaningful and justifiable symbolic representations of that reality that nature has provided for the welfare, sustenance and protection of all living creatures. If humans wish to kill and torture themselves and to destroy nature, then it is humans that are perverted. If humans are natural perverts, then as for every natural ill there is a natural cure then only universally correct cultures can cure humanity.

Universally correct cultures are those intellectual constructs that provide the logical and rational framework by which all acts can be tested to see if they conform to those objective and independent principles of proper and correct conduct that time and human conscience have shown to be indispensable in forming worthwhile, meaningful and productive living conditions for all living creatures. From such reasoning universally acceptable culturally correct and proper conclusions can become those essential attributes that are deemed necessary to accompany man throughout his time upon this planet. Being essential necessities they are in fact absolute cultural necessities or cultural absolutes. Cultural absolutes are those entities that are the natural product of the intellect acting upon what nature has given man so that all men can conclude that which is fair, just and worthwhile and what is perverse, worthless and thus evil.

If throughout time all men arrive at the same cultural conclusions, then these conclusions become inalienable in that they exist independent to time and are the birthright of all living creatures. Those cultural conclusions that are absolutely necessary to maintain the intellectual honour and dignity of man being axiomatic form the basis of all subordinate disciplines and belief systems. Thus, the cultural axioms of a nation are represented by the religious affairs and then the political affairs of that nation. Accordingly, all religions and political systems are not only subordinate to universally applicable cultures they are also dependent upon them to act as criteria against which their action can be judged.

These cultural codes are essential to curb the more outlandish manifestations of intellectual stupidity that are endemic to bigoted religious and political systems that always tend to attract the more disaffected and morally dysfunctional sections of societies.

Thus universally applicable cultures which possess well defined criteria to assess the correct behaviour of its subordinates as well as having the cultural constancy necessary to enforce those cultural contracts necessary to ensure fairness and justice must also be prepared to issue all and any individual who subscribes to the culture by freely submitting to its laws an individual cultural indemnity card which lists what that individual can expect to receive from that culture to which they have attached themselves.

This entitlement and indemnity card would clearly state from which harms the possessor would be secured from and would list the benefits to which they were entitled.

Cultures become great and constant by being seen to be fair and just. Being above religious, political and economic affairs, they can issue interdicts to ensure the independence and validity of their individual indemnity permits.

These permits not only declare the cultural status of the holder they also ensure that the individual is given a cultural copyright that cannot morally or ethically be used or abused by another for gain or profit. Such permits would allow the individual to enter into independent cultural contracts and would record the honourable status of the holder so that others could assess their worthiness.

The conclusions arrived at by the intellect concerning how man should progress towards his destiny form the basis of all cultures. However, there is, in fact, only one culture. This single cultural entity exists as an independent absolute which can only be described one way. Also, it can only be predicated one way. It is therefore described as being right and prescribed as being true. Any intellectual construct that is both right and true and which is further enhanced by time proving it to be a proper and fair construct that is meaningful and useful in dealing with reality must therefore not only be independent to time but must also be independent to particular places, particular societies and particular belief systems.

Culture means to grow – but to grow into what? The word describes the process not the end result. It describes a stage in the intellectual evolution of man towards an objective. What is this objective and how can it be described and thence prescribed as being a worthy one? Religion calls this God; politics call it the 'self'. However, it is in fact an everlasting process – the culture of creativity in which a single absolute intellectual construct can only be described and prescribed one way yet its meaning to each and every one can be expressed in many forms. Accordingly, the culture of creativity or simply creation is what is being discussed. Creation, because it is the purpose of man, is inviolable. Anything that acts against this purpose is therefore evil.

Creation and creativity are independent realities that will continue to exist only if men continue to create. It is up to true men to create a new universal culture in which all have a place and a space to fulfil their natural creative functioning. It is up to true men to create a culture which indemnifies each and every individual against those evil and perverted parasitic organisms that have been specially selected by the jealousy of greed to inflict as much harm and distress upon nature and its products as is feasibly possible.

In a creative culture it is the individual who represents the intellectual cultural constructs that form the laws which govern how that society and nation is to function. The laws of such nations therefore reside in the individual and not in some ethereal no man's land. The laws are prescriptive and therefore possess no relative or subordinate descriptive clauses. Being culturally prescriptive laws, they are absolute laws and thus universally applicable. Being absolute universally applicable laws which inhere in the individual subjected to the cultural contracts of a nation means that every individual is free in the one true meaning of the word – that is the individual represents the laws of their adopted culture and is therefore free to express themselves in any manner that is fit and proper to the meaning and value of that culture. One therefore has one's culture, then one's religion then one's political ideas, then social and domestic concerns – but it is one's culture that empowers and protects the individual for no other thing can or should.

A strong creative culture would protect the individual from those interfering busybodies who squander vast amounts of resources in a never-ending quest to terrorise all living creatures into submitting to their one world doctrine of domination, segregation and division into politically classified dependent groups of disenfranchised state-owned individuals whose sole purpose in existence is to support the state, no matter the cost to humanity.

A strong creative culture would issue all its members with a cultural indemnity card which would entitle the holder to food, shelter and warmth and freedom from state interference or harm as an absolute right.

A strong creative culture would state that each of its individuals is a representative of the laws of that culture and as such cannot be interfered with or held without objective evidence. Thus, that vile, jealous drivel that always drips from the lips of the greedy, the disaffected or the emotionally unstable would not constitute objective evidence – nor the politically motivated fear of the parasitic that their distortion of reality has been detected could be used to detain such people. Accordingly the predilection of the political perverts and their paid hirelings to pounce upon anyone or anything at the slightest hint of political incorrectness and have them locked up – just in case – could be dispensed with and seen for what it is – the hysterical over-reaction of a sick society in case its own perversions, whilst eagerly being indulged in, are seen by others to be given the approval of the political and social bigots who control it.

Individual assaults upon the honour and integrity of an individual protected by a strong and creative culture, if proved to have arisen through malice, wilful ignorance or idleness, would result in the accuser or accusers being held responsible by them being subjected to a punishment equal to that which the accused would have been liable to.

Only in strong creative cultures with the concept of equal reciprocity can an individual be completely free from idle and malicious interference. Strong creative cultures therefore codify those laws necessary for the correct functioning of its members. This codex would list the necessary cultural contracts that time has proved must exist between individual members of that culture if they are to function in a productive and harmonious fashion and in a manner which is natural to them.

If such a culture is to function correctly each of its members must agree to be bound by the codes of conduct that are necessary for its health and wellbeing.

In strong creative cultures no individual has any individual rights that would put them in a position of superiority over another individual – they only possess universal rights which define in cultural terms what is right and proper for each and every individual. Thus, if some greedy pig wishes to stand in the trough guzzling at one end whilst polluting it for the rest from the other then a strong creative culture would soon remove such an obscenity.

However, in sick and diseased societies without any cultural cohesion such obscene excesses are viewed with a type of detached envy.

Strong and creative cultures generate independent cultural absolutes which can be adopted by any individual. These cultural absolutes are superior to and are unaffected by religious or political doctrines. They exist independently to life, or any particular interpretation of what existence means. They transcend reality for they are the very basis upon which all rational thoughts depend.

They are above the power of any god or creator for they would exist even without existence.

It is in reality too late for any power whatsoever to change what is. A popular philosophical statement that unites the active and the passive states,

'I think therefore I am.'

But this statement goes too far for the self that thinks may only think the thoughts of others and the self thus created is simply a clone who drones to the same tune as all the other deluded creatures.

What can be said that cannot be denied is 'something was'. No sooner are we aware of anything that it becomes the past. It is a retrospective reasoning that decides what the something was.

But true men wish to be creative and not only to state that 'something was ' -they wish to state that 'something was – and it was good.' It is the duty of true men to create a creative culture of which any creator would state that it was good.

As has been stated good means well balanced that is fair and wholesome.

Look about you. What is well balanced, fair and wholesome upon this planet?

Independent cultural absolutes are the birth rite of all living creatures whether they are aware of them or not. They grant to every living creature the moral and ethical right to live unmolested by the malignant interfering parasitic organisms that infest life with their grotesque intellectual inadequacies.

True men must exist to grant every living creature the moral and ethical right to live unmolested by others. They do this by creating strong creative cultures that freely grant those who wish to be governed by the cultural contracts and codes of conduct necessary to its validity, a symbol of their cultural status that others interfere with at their peril.

Thus, those vicious wretches who stalk the corridors of cruelty inflicting their insane and deformed ideas of what constitutes dignified behaviour upon the defenceless and enslaved are the offspring of sick and deformed cultures supported by a debased and dysfunctional society who empower parasitic and feeble-minded democratic dictators to wreak their uncontrollable rage upon anyone or anything beyond their control.

Each and every living creature has an absolute and unalterable universal right to protect themselves and to be protected from that self-interest interference that is the trademark of the intellectually and emotionally unstable.

No living creature has the right to directly or indirectly interfere with another one. True men must therefore create a culture and a society in which those hysterical outbursts of those intellectually inadequate parasitic maggots who would pass for our guardians are treated with the contempt they deserve. True men must ensure that no man is subjected to the hysterical screeching of malignant hags who have been empowered by the parasitic maggots to destroy any and all creative movements that might threaten the perpetuity of decadent democratic systems of misgovernment.

One can close one's eyes. One can close one's mouth, but no one can close their ears. Thus, an incessant and perpetual campaign of political drivel must be enacted every minute of the day in order that all items of news must consist not of cultural affairs but of the latest antics of the deformed democracies that enslave true men.

Without a strong creative culture, we are nothing. In fact, we are worse than nothing we are selfish, greedy individuals who seek only to harm ourselves and others.

The role of true men is to ensure that every existent being has a proper purpose within life and to harm or distort that purpose is a cultural crime.

To achieve their creative potential all living creatures must be granted those absolute cultural rights that are independent to and of political, social or religious interference.

These absolute cultural rights state that every living creature has the absolute right to live unmolested by other creatures. Every living creature has the absolute right to food, shelter and warmth. Every living creature has the absolute right to enter into a cultural contract with others and that the contract so formed is above those political and religious laws because all political and religious systems are subordinate and subservient to cultural laws.

If therefore any individual, group, company, nation or culture interferes in the affairs of another culture for political or religious reasons then the aggressors are acting illegitimately and are therefore cultural outlaws.

Each individuated existent being owns their own cultural copyright. To abuse or damage that copyright in any manner whatsoever is a cultural crime and therefore an illegal act.

Thus, cultural outlaws are dishonourable cultural outlaws that have lost those universal rights to be protected by any independent cultural absolutes and thus become legitimate targets for intellectual ridicule and social banishment.

Every individuated existent being owns a specific and natural share of this planet. No authority can usurp an individual entities rights to wholesome food, unadulterated by scientific profiteers, inept and deformed governments or greedy producers.

No agency whatsoever can deny an individual access to shelter.

No authority can deny any individual the right to gather to themselves those objects required for warmth.

No individual has the right to pollute the living space of another by noise, sight, smell or toxins.

Those absolute rights require nothing from the individual for they are inherent in the individual themselves.

Therefore, all those individuals that subscribe to a strong creative culture that grants them inalienable cultural absolute rights are granted that essential freedom from those physical, emotional, intellectual, social and economic pollutants that accompany all diseased and degenerate democracies that bulldoze their way towards nowhere. Of these it may only be said 'Something was – and it was bad!'

Degenerate democracies however need to pretend to be culturally aware and active. They therefore create a culture founded upon that exclusivity that results from perverted power enslaving and interfering with others for profit and that delights in interfering with its victims. Accordingly degenerate democracies invent distorted political systems that pander to those popular perversions that will ensure the parasitic remain in power. Thus, a popular culture arises that ensures that only those political principles that uphold the validity of their own perversions are permissible. This ensures that democratic dictatorships spring up which terrified at their own transience cast around wildly to ensure that all their acts are in accordance with the statistical evidence of what constitutes the latest fashionable fetish.

After a short time a thoroughly depressing picture of abnormality emerges as democratic decency degenerates into a sort of dictatorial pornocratic timocracy in which each political parasite's actions are dictated to by the warmongers, the money junkies and the control freaks and having been elected upon the profits of profligacy they feel obliged to prostitute themselves, their conscience and their ideals in order to support their own pathetic political party.

Such political and cultural parasites delight in the exclusivity afforded by their denial of the rights of others. They therefore aspire to be at the forefront of their popular culture which states numerical superiority is all that matters and thus they end up owning an obscene number of slums into which they pour those aliens that have had to be imported to keep their rot boxes full and their outlandish vehicles polished.

Those surplus to requirements intellectual and moral inadequates should be consigned to that history that awaits all vicious and vindictive interfering scum that wish to own this world. It is the job of true men to create some forgotten hole in the middle of nowhere into which to tip this riff raff so that they may defile and degrade each other with their cultural and spiritual insignificance.

In a world with leaders ever ready to prostitute themselves to the promiscuity of political popularism strong and creative cultures are often deliberately destroyed in order that the societies that depended upon them to keep honesty, integrity, honour and justice alive may be enslaved and subjugated to a new one world ordering.

When honour, integrity, honesty and justice become subservient to political expediency then life itself becomes a meaningless and pointless exercise because the inherent inconstancy of political ideologies ensure that no stability is possible.

When a culture dies so do the morals of its peoples. Understanding is replaced by wilful ignorance and forgiveness is for fools. Humanity for other creatures disappears in a scientific frenzy to immortalise the decaying carcases of such sick societies by enacting vast programmes of research in ways to inflict unimaginable suffering in the lives of other living creatures in the futile and forlorn hope of extending the miserable and pointless lives of those living in a culturally dead society.

Sick societies sensing their own ethical squalor enact campaigns of vicious hatred and jealous spite against all others who have not succumbed to their tarnished and tainted political systems.

Nations and their politics that pander to the intellectually inadequate numerical quantification of worthiness are in fact perverted for they pander to all those who wish to be numerically superior to all others no matter the cost to humanity, who are eligible to vote no matter how intellectually or morally dysfunctional, who think nothing of slaughtering the unborn, who believe they have the right to be unbelievably stupid and inept, who glorify the thugs and henchmen that the system empowers to murder others, who think that education consists of learning numbers and words and who are ever keen to see vast amounts of the world's resources squandered on a perpetual process of medical madness that attempts to produce perfectly polished people who positively shine in their attempt to mask the spiritual stench of their mangled minds as they dribble away their existences in a pit of cultural isolation and loneliness because they belong to the state and the state for all its pompous proclamations treats them like the mindless factory fodder that they have become.

14 The Order of Cultural Controls

Cultural Contracts and Laws
Culturally Enforced Codes of Conduct
Culturally Aware and Creative Citizens
Civil Service
Religious and Spiritual Societies
Political Movements and Governments

IF POLITICAL MOVEMENTS and their governors attempt to deny their subordinate role within civilised societies then there is a danger that they become uncontrollable for they quickly become a sectarian band of self-appointing elitists who wish to control and dominate every aspect of life. They then accrue to themselves and their supporters' powers – powers that they do not naturally or ethically possess, and these culturally illegitimate powers inevitably lead to humanitarian abuses because usurped illegitimate powers display no moral restraint when challenged by legitimate questions as to their validity.

It may be seen that for a society to function correctly all religious and spiritual movements as well as political ones must be made subordinate and subservient to the cultural contracts, laws and codes of conduct of a nation. This is necessary in order to avoid the type of sectarian bigoted violence that arises when one individual or sect believe themselves to be superior to others through belonging to a class of person favoured by some sort of deity for some obscure reason best known to themselves who has chosen them rather someone else. Such mythologies arise when religions usurp the role of intelligent universal cultural constructs.

Any creator worth their salt would, like a good parent, make all their offspring equal to the task for which they were created. Furthermore, any intelligent creator would only create that which is necessary for their purpose to be fulfilled and therefore each and every created creature is to them of equal worth. All cohesive cultures recognise the need for a diversity of purpose and that every living creature has a unique task and forms an essential and irreplaceable link in that great chain of being. If any link within that chain becomes isolated or enslaved or abused for the amusement or profit of another then life and existence itself becomes perverted and debased.

If all living creatures have a particular and unique purpose, then all must be treated equally. We all have our own pictures to paint, and each individual picture is necessary to build up and complete the jigsaw of life. If just one piece is missing, then the whole is spoilt. Accordingly, to discriminate against anyone for any reason is absurd unless they are actively seeking to destroy or debase the culture to which they belong or attempt to debase or destroy a culture that is not their concern.

If therefore you discover that your national or local governors are using arbitrary methods of their own creation to assess individual needs according to gender, physical status, age or political or environmental circumstances then they are acting in a culturally illegitimate and discriminatory manner.

Such artificially imposed discriminatory measures are in fact cultural crimes for they perpetuate a dangerous and divisive belief that one section of society deserves to be treated preferentially and thus differently from another. This type of political bigotry leads towards social structures that assess every individual against some inconsistent and discriminatory arbitrary scale that must and does vary from one locality to another.

But in our journey towards our individual destinies, we all have our cross to bear. In cohesive cultures each of its members are treated as one connected mass all moving towards a common goal and thus it would be culturally absurd to single out one group or another for some transient political expedient.

However, in culturally dead societies with intellectually challenged systems the state concentrates almost exclusively upon classifying its citizens into arbitrarily constructed sections and divisions and then feels obliged to squander vast amounts of a nation's resources in an attempt to cure the incurable and to miseducate the dysfunctional in order to create by legislation a nation that accords with their distorted ideas of what existence is all about.

One may ask, 'What is going on?'

Well basically because the state needs to control and order its citizens around so that they conform to some arbitrarily constructed ideal of what a nation should be like they embark upon a campaign of thuggery and theft so that all those intellectual and physical freedoms essential for constructing strong and creative and cohesive cultures in which all are considered to be of equal worth and in which all are welcome to participate upon equal terms no matter how intellectually or physically disabled are no longer recognised as being an individual's copyright and thus all nationals are considered to be state owned and controlled property. The degree of participation within the life of that nation is then controlled by the state and thus the state and happiness of a nation is directly under the control of its political system. If that political system rejects those universal cultural and control values that are essential to compensate for the transient unstable nature of such organisations, then a self-perpetuating dictatorial political elite will arise that will invade and interfere with every aspect of a nation's life.

Great cultures are aware that there can be no real happiness without participation, and they therefore formulate their educatory systems to teach all individuals their intellectual and cultural heritage so that they avoid becoming confused and isolated links and unable to participate because they lack a sense of their own worth.

Strong cohesive all-inclusive cultures link every living organism together to form one great chain of participation each link being culturally aware of their worth.

What then is the purpose of such a chain? The chain itself is the purpose of existence. Once the final link is in place then life itself has fulfilled its purpose. Logic and philosophy tell us that we do not in fact require a body or other material form to exist as sentient intelligent beings. Some distant catastrophic event occurred that made the materialisation of existence itself essential. The damage done to our spiritual and intellectual lives let alone our physical ones is evident for all to see.

It is the job of all existent creatures to work together to repair the damage done by this cataclysm. To do this one great universal all-inclusive culture must be created to reunite mankind in order that they may heal that festering wound that will weep forever unless we act together. That festering wound is kept open and sore by that proud jealous greed that belongs to all those who consider themselves superior and special. If men create a culture in which all have equal status, then life itself will heal itself naturally. Each individual will then act for the common good of all and each person will then be free to transcend the limitations of their own souls and become an integral and integrated part of one great universal chain of being.

It is the job of perverted politicians and their henchmen to destroy all cohesive cultures in order that each member of humanity becomes an isolated link that can be used and abused for profit. Like dumb animals they are fed a never-ending diet of political propaganda and kept in check by financial and social terrorists who daily threaten to disenfranchise anyone who does not bow down to the state.

Such is the political pollution of our culture there are few if any places left where we can escape from our daily diet of debauched practices.

One can close one's eyes so as to avoid watching their antics and one can walk away from their confrontational attitude but one cannot close one's ears to those who cry out for our help and assistance.

The worst form of abuse is noise abuse, and the worst form of noise abuse is verbal abuse. But we are made to suffer either at the hands of malignant hormonally challenged emotionally unstable hags who delight in regurgitating the puerile puss that dribbles from the mouths of intellectually subnormal deranged dictators or in our attempt to discover what is going on are confronted by a media who transmit messages made meaningless because they consist almost entirely of non-essential facts and figures.

It is not the age of a person, their marital or financial status, nor the number of days or the date or how many guns were used or how many bullets were fired. It is not their height or weight or their appearance or race or religion or who said what or how many nations are in shock or what the perverted politicians say or how many new laws will be passed or what the polls say or how many voted or how many more henchmen will be required nor whether they live in a detached, semi-detached, terraced or caravan nor what they were wearing nor the colour of their car nor how long they worked at the pie factory nor what the leader of the opposition thinks nor what the man in the street has to say nor the number of times the item is repeated, nor on how many channels – it is why each person did what they did – it is the meaning of their actions and that which caused them to act in such a way that is important.

It is the culture of a nation that explains to its people why they or others act in the way that they do.

Without a culture in control all reported acts remain inexplicable and random.

A nation with a strong all-inclusive and creative culture will possess people who act in a civilised and friendly manner.

The culture of a nation is not primarily expressed or contained in its music, its pictures or its writings. It is expressed through its people, through their faces. It is expressed through and how its people lead their daily lives. It is expressed in the way its people treat themselves, each other and other people.

15 Cultural Truths, Contracts and Credit Cards

TRUE MEANS STRAIGHT – not devious, corrupt, perverse or depraved. True also implies constancy for if anything is to be considered true then it requires that this truth never changes or alters. Truths that never or cannot alter are objective or absolute truths. For example, an absolute or objective truth is that yellow plus blue make green. This book is also concerned with the other types of truth that exist. For instance, there are contingent truths that is contingent upon the facts at hand. A wall may be green and if it is then this a contingent truth – a wall does not have to be any colour to be a wall – it just so happens to be the case. Relative truths relate to relationships between objects or events. The ball may be near the dustbin, but this is not a necessary truth for either the ball or the bin.

Political systems deal exclusively in contingent and relative truths. Cultural systems deal exclusively with objective and essential truths. Accordingly, politicians can lie and cheat until the cows come home yet they cannot be held to account because of the inherent transient nature of their tenure upon political life.

Cultural systems cannot cheat and lie without destroying themselves for they deal almost exclusively in objective that is universal truths which cannot and do not change with time or fashion. One constantly recurring truth that cultures have to deal with is that human nature and its needs do not alter with time. But human nature has two different and differing components – male and female. Like water which is composed of two very different and volatile elements they must be brought together with great care and attention but once united form an exceedingly stable and essential compound.

Accordingly, a form of cultural contract is necessary to recognise that if such different elements or organisms are not brought together with care and consideration then only disaster will occur.

To safeguard man's cultural creditworthiness and honour it is essential that a contract is drawn up which recognises that when two different objects come together, they are very vulnerable and susceptible to all sorts of unwanted attention, distraction and interference.

One of the most important cultural ties that can be undertaken is that in which two different and differing people unite together to form a union by and through which their culture and their society is enabled to renew itself and move towards its ultimate purpose. By producing offspring that can be raised and educated in those universal principles of justice, equality and fairness those who are united using that authority that only universally applicable cultures can legitimately possess can and do create strong and cohesive cultures that lead to great civilisations.

The cultural contract of marriage is essential to a man for two major reasons. Man is one of the very few if not the only animal that does not have an automatic rigid trigger mechanism in his reproductive organ. He is therefore dependent upon visual and sensual stimuli in order to be aroused. Furthermore, chemicals in his brain suspend his intellectual and reasoning capacity to such an extent that he reverts to being a wild irrational animal.

Accordingly, he is extremely vulnerable at this stage for he cannot be said to be acting rationally. Once aroused very little if anything can stop or persuade him from not fulfilling his natural creative function.

It is therefore the duty of his culture to ensure that he is fully protected at this vulnerable stage by the construction of codes of conduct that everyone should respect in order that he is not taken advantage of by others.

The second essential reason for having a cultural contract is that the process of reproduction takes many years to mature into a meaningful relationship.

Very few if any wedding nights are nights of unbridled passion – they are simply the beginning of a long and emotionally expensive journey in which both parties discover the ultimate futility of attempting to deny nature for if nature does not have its way it will destroy those that mock it.

Accordingly, strife and division naturally arise. Physical and verbal abuse become commonplace domestic activities.

But such common and inevitable everyday occurrences that are the necessary and natural methods by and through which different relationships are reformed and recreated are now no longer considered those necessary transient traumas that affect all living creatures, be it man or beast, but are politicised into the public domain.

But the public domain in sick societies is one in which there is a depraved fascination for the physical and thus any and every act of physical aggression at home is treated with that shock horror irrational and hysterical fright that mirrors the emotional and intellectual instability of those culturally dead societies who, though they think nothing of slaughtering other nations or their own unborn, fly into a fit of self-righteous indignation and call upon the state and its henchmen to interfere in order to assuage their own perverted guilt at allowing their perverted politicians to get away with murder.

Cultural contacts must therefore possess a constancy of purpose so that those who enter into them are made fully aware of what to expect and as they are constant contracts, how long they must expect it.

But such contracts are binding in honour only. In societies that lack honour, and which display a complete contempt for shame there is always an abundance of slimy solicitors touting their tatty trade who are keen to see the first signs of friction and dissent so that they may profit from interfering in those domestic issues that are none of their concern.

Domestic issues are cultural concerns, and it is the job of creative cultures to sort our civil and domestic strife. But domestic and civil strife are by and large politically generated states of affairs.

If all living creatures were treated as if they were of equal worth and value and were granted absolute rights, then there would be little left to cause disputes.

There are many cultural outlets for those jealous rages that people fly into but in sick and deformed societies suffering under dictatorial elitist democracies they no longer are permitted to exist so that people are forced to turn against each other in a sickening dance to the death of their relationship which only profits slimy solicitors and social workers.

Decadent democracies delight in seeing their societies and culture torn apart and thus they pass as many divisive laws as possible in order that they may appear to be indispensable in running and ordering society which through their interference is no longer capable of running or ordering itself.

With regard to the education of people it may be appreciated that great care and attention is required in formulating the cultural contracts that all students must enter into in order that they may be taught those disciplines which are essential for them to develop into well balanced, culturally aware and active members of a nation.

If they learn that no single human authority has the right to interfere with them in their quest to learn those things which are essential for the health of their intellects, then they need not tolerate noisy unruly students who only wish to re-enact the antics of their favourite cartoon characters and the role models in their cartoon culture.

Accordingly, any student no matter of what class, no matter in which type of establishment who deliberately disrupts another can be legitimately removed for the cultural rights of the individual are absolute rights and not political or numerical ones.

Cultural contracts which state the rights of every individual student are essential in avoiding the miseducation of those who are vulnerable and sensitive to verbal and physical abuse.

The culture of a nation is represented by and through the protection it affords to every one of its citizens.

The culture of a nation forms the moral and ethical foundation of and justification for its laws and codes of conduct.

All citizens who belong to a nation that possesses a creative and cohesive culture would be entitled to a cultural credit card that grants to that citizen the absolute rights that all living creatures upon this planet are entitled to.

For instance:

The absolute right to life from the moment of conception.

The absolute right to food, shelter and warmth.

The absolute right to live free from political, social and environmental interference.

The absolute right to defend themselves and their culture from depraved and decadent perverts.

The absolute right to possess their own unique cultural copyright that cannot be used or abused by anyone for any reason whatsoever.

The absolute right to have all those cultural contracts freely entered into honoured and respected by all subordinate and subservient political and religious organisations.

It is the absolute right of every individual to be issued at birth with a cultural credit card that not only identifies them but grants them indemnity against abuse and grants them complete and absolute control over their own copyright.

If they honour their cultural heritage and remain in credit by not cheating, lying or defrauding their fellow citizens and if they refuse to use and abuse others for power and profit then they will be treated with that respect and honour that can only be true and meaningful if it is bestowed by a disinterested and universally recognised authority.

If you live in a nation that does not possess any cultural authority and therefore cannot issue you with a legitimate cultural identity or credit card, then if you wish to be a true man then use your creative and intellectual abilities to establish a strong and cohesive culture.

Such a culture if it proves to be universally applicable and readily understandable and if it also is founded upon those just and fair principles by and through which others can benefit then it will bear the necessary cultural authority to care for and protect its members. Furthermore, its laws and codes of conduct can be used to control the self-interested excesses endemic to religious and political systems that have at their very foundations the belief that one living creature can be superior to another.

No intelligent rational being would consider such a proposition to be valid for it is like stating that red is superior to blue or that one musical note is more important than another.

Great cultures and civilisations arise when they understand and recognise that for the truth we require every colour, shade and hue, the combinations of which are unlimited and that we require every note and every sound and every chord in order that the whole purpose of our existence is achieved when every living creature is allowed to fulfil its purpose and the final piece of the jigsaw is permitted to be freely and unconditionally put into its proper place. Only civilised creative and cohesive cultures can direct us towards the order in which the pieces fit together, and it is only great all-inclusive cultures that can give us a glimpse of what that final picture of reality looks like.

16 Illegitimate Cultural Reforms

LEGITIMACY CAN ONLY arise when there is a universal apperception that that which has come before the intellect of a rationally coherent creature is judged to be a universally acceptable and beneficial idea relative to all other living creatures.

Accordingly legitimate acts are well balanced universally acceptable and beneficial and thus justifiable upon ethical grounds in that they are good, that is, well balanced well thought out intellectual constructs.

However, to be universally legitimate acts human intellectual constructs must be based upon those objective and universal truths that are independent to time, traditions and the transient religious and political trammels of the day.

Objective truths that have become universal truths by the passage of time are those truths that cannot be denied without those who deny them having a sense of shame and dishonour that no matter how disguised makes them sick at heart because they become aware that they have denied their own rationality and humanity for the sake of some temporary and transient expediency.

Objective means what all men who display a disinterest in the temporary, transient and selfish interests generated by jealous greed would consider to be a fair and just idea, concept or proposition.

If throughout time men reach the same conclusions as to what constitutes justice and fairness, then those human intellectually constructed ideas become universalised and become universal truths.

Furthermore, universal truths being objective truths are not only independent of time they are also independent to any particular sect or group and therefore become absolute truths that is non contingent truths because they exist as independent unconditional and unalterable realities.

These universal truths form the basis of all cultures and religions and therefore are the ethical standards by and through which all acts can be judged to assess their justice and fairness. Justice therefore is independent to individual, sects, groups, societies or even nations.

Accordingly, it is those universally acceptable intellectual constructs which have as their foundation universal and objective truths that form the basis for the legitimacy of those acts and intentions that govern the running of a nation.

Even if all nations degenerated into debased egotistical manifestations of greed, pride, avarice and debauchery and spent their time upon this planet destroying it and themselves, those actions no matter how universally adopted and practised, could not constitute any rational threat to the meaning, purpose and validity of those universally applicable intellectual constructs that form cohesive and creative cultures.

As has been stated intelligence is limited, that is its boundaries are set and fixed by cultural criteria of what is and what isn't sensible. Stupidity is unlimited and without strong intellectually valid coherent cultures it will continue to despoil and destroy not only all cultures but human values and ultimately humanity itself.

Nature has provided mankind with the ability to construct creative and coherent cultures which generate codes of conduct which are expressed by its members in how they live their lives and the meaning and validity they attach to those cultural contracts that time has demonstrated are essential for the formation of stable, cohesive, constant and content societies that are indispensable for the civilisation of those wild emotionally charged creatures known as humans.

Further, to recognise the validity and justification for living by such codes and practices, that spiritual affiliation that all humans share with nature, that very nature that has freed their minds from the slavery and drudgery of instinctive and often irrational actions, is recognised by assigning a religious ceremony which binds those essential contracts by demanding that those so bound honour their cultural commitment.

That is what religion means – to bind. Religions therefore cannot in themselves be the cause of conflict, but degenerate sectarian divisive and intellectually deficient and morally bankrupt cultures certainly can be and are.

However, cultures require not only a method to bind and sanctify contracts, which means to make whole (and thus complete and rational) they need a group of servers to enact and conduct these codes of conduct and to act as guardians for their national cultural heritage to ensure that their culture, its codes and its contracts are being honoured.

These cultural servers are known as civil servers or servants because they are charged with keeping daily life in a civilised order. It is the job of elected representatives to ensure that the daily order of life is kept as stable and constant as possible so that people may go about their daily tasks without any illegal, unnecessary, illegitimate or idle official or unofficial interference.

Such elected representatives are known as politicians. Accordingly in the natural order of civilised life we have a cohesive inclusive coherent culture which generates codes of conduct and contractual laws which are bound and made whole by religious orders which further oversee and control the civil servants who are duty bound to see that those cultural laws and contacts are honoured. Then we have politicians who are elected by the citizens of a nation to ensure that their daily lives remain stable and constant.

Thus, the elected representatives of a nation are dealing exclusively in contingent truths – that is truths that are dependent upon daily circumstance. They are dealing with subjective truths for political systems are fractionalised into sects and parties each with their own subjects – those policies which form the political agenda as published in their manifestos.

They are thus dealing exclusively in synthetic truths – that is truths that arise out of combining differing and diverse elements to form a whole and thus synthetic truths are not only contingent truths, contingent upon which political ingredients have been mixed together, they become relative truths which are relevant only to the party politics of that sectarian grouping.

But subjective truths cannot replace objective truths, and contingent upon the times truths cannot compete with universal truths and relative truths composed of a hotchpotch of diverse opinions and ideas cannot be compared with absolute or analytic truths.

Politicians are therefore dealing exclusively in arbitrary and expedient thus expendable truths. Being arbitrary, expedient and expendable truths, they possess no cultural universal legitimacy and when they attempt to overturn, alter or interfere with those universally acceptable absolute noncontingent objective analytic truths that form the basis for all coherent and creative cultures that are essential for the formation of a civilised planet they are acting illegitimately.

What qualification does one require to be an elected representative of the people? Is one required to spend decades studying those necessary, logical and intellectual constructs that empower an individual to wisely choose between truths and those falsehoods and fallacies that can so easily arise when an individual confuses one type of truth with and for another? Are such representatives required to demonstrate the ability to be adept and skilful in prescribing and describing how and in what manner the geometric conversions of those universally acceptable intellectual constructs, formulated in a brutal and debased language, are going to be transformed into worthwhile, beneficial and cohesive public policies whilst at the same time respecting and honouring those cultural and religious traditions that make one nation discernible from another?

Politicians simply cannot and do not possess the intellectual capacity nor any legitimacy to alter or interfere with a culture, its codes of conduct or its contracts.

Politicians are in fact superfluous to civilised life and were only introduced to curb the power of one pornocracy but have ended up creating another.

The electronic revolution now enables the citizens of most nations to issue direct mandates to their civil servants to enact those policies necessary for the orderly and smooth running of their societies.

But if those citizens have been subjected to years of cultural miseducation and politically motivated abuse then the transformation from one political system to another will be delayed and postponed until all members of that nation are given the absolute cultural rights necessary for them to function as truly free and capable political agents.

It is the job of all citizens to create a strong and cohesive culture, and it is the job of all true men to use their unique creative abilities to demonstrate how a nation can regain control of its commonwealth and humanity and thus return life itself to fulfilling its proper meaning and purpose.

Just as politics need to be subordinated to the culture of a nation so must its religions. Religions are those adopted ceremonial constructs that allow people to collectively witness those cultural contracts that are necessary to uphold the honour and integrity of societies.

Religions cannot and were never meant to be intellectually valid logical constructs.

No god or creator could or can deny that once the intellect has been granted to human life that it would be possible to change it. Created life has a constancy and a purpose that cannot and does not change. A square will always be a set figure with a fixed proportion. If it were to alter then it would become something else, but the idea and the concept of a square would always remain. Once established by the mind even if all life were to cease one could always truly state that 'something was, and it was square.' No power could or would wish to alter the ratio of one side to another and no power could or would alter how the intellect functions within man.

Religions do not deal with fixed and constant ratios. Religions do not deal with absolute truths. Religions deal in prophecies and in that faith which must of necessity exist if those things which are prophesised are to be believable. Great religions arise not out of the prophets themselves but out of their teachings. Prophets that attempt to universalise their own beliefs by claiming to be directly sent from their fathers claim only that which all men can claim for we are all sons, we are all equal, we are therefore all equally worthy to be prophets, to be sons of God, to be saviours.

Accordingly, no religion can claim an exclusivity to pontificate upon how best to conduct one's life, yet all religions agree that it is how the individual behaves and what their intentions are that forms the basis upon which their worthiness to share in the next stages of man's journey through existence is to be judged.

Thus, all religions require their members to have a faith that is a trust in the future of the individual self as a distinct and discernible entity that can and will be recognised in a non-material form. However, religions in and by themselves cannot grant any absolute credits or honours because even the saintliest may harbour a heart of black hatred and despair and a soul riddled with perverse and malignant intentions.

It is only the culture of a nation that can truly recognise and honour individuals with the credit that they deserve and even in spite of their own failings and limitations for great cultures are designed and created to transcend the physical and mental weaknesses of their members by abstracting and keeping the good whilst at the same time rejecting and ridiculing the bad.

Great cultures therefore are discriminatory so that when they are faced with that whole rotting mess of humanity, they are able to discern what is fair, just and sensible and select that which is good whilst rejecting that which is evil.

Any nation therefore that does not create or possess universal cultural values can never be considered a truly democratic one.

Without a comprehensive system of educating all people into a state of knowing and understanding universal cultural values, how they arise and how to use them and their intellects to discriminate between different types of truths and the different forms of reasoning available to the mind they will remain unable to fully exercise their right to live and work in and under a truly democratic system of governance.

What then is a truly democratic system of governance?

Democracy means the strength of the people, but if those very people are sick and dysfunctional, miseducated and politically and socially isolated then what power can they legitimately exercise?

But in every generation, there arises a new breed of person who, if they avoid being slaughtered in some vicious war of jealous greed and hatred, realise that all is not well with this planet.

They begin to believe that they will never be able to alter this world for the power to do so lies elsewhere and outside their control.

Fair Play

In some nations their cultures are founded upon a system of living known as 'fair play'.

No matter the game it is understood that all may take part and that no single individual is to receive preferential treatment – no matter how disadvantaged.

This system ensures that each is allotted their role according to their natural abilities and not according to some arbitrary contingent emotional empathetic reasoning that some players have to be surgically, chemically, electronically or financially enhanced and empowered in order that the disabled are enabled and the paralytic promoted to positions that are unsuitable for them and everyone else, irrespective of whether they are intellectually, morally, socially or physically disadvantaged. Fair play, that inherent balance between capabilities and positioning is further enhanced by the aims and aspirations of all the participants being in a realistic accordance with their chances of success.

It is the culture of a nation that is charged with ensuring a level playing field, with goals and targets of equal dimensions, of rules and regulations to ensure proper behaviour and conduct and a team of artisans and trainers to ensure that everyone is aware of what they need to do, how to do it, what is not required of them, what is expected of them and most importantly to enjoy themselves and enter into the spirit of the game.

Without cultural guidance the game of life becomes a meaningless, pointless and unenjoyable scramble for individual glory and success wherein trampling upon the faces of others in order to achieve one's goal is what it's all about.

It is the culture of a nation that ensures that all who participate are educated to be aware of those necessary and inevitable cuts and bruises, broken noses and sore heads that come with taking up a position that one might not be fit enough to adopt.

In sick societies which lack cultural cohesion and guidance the intellectually, emotionally and morally disabled are always pushed to the front of the queue from whence they are shoehorned into inappropriate positions. This particularly embarrassing form of intellectually inadequate, dogmatic and divisive politically motivated stupidity is necessary to ensure that those who are truly capable of ensuring fair and just play are sidelined into making tea and scones for the half-time interval.

An inevitable result of such stupidity is that such ill-advised interference in the lives' hopes and aspirations of those budding prima donnas who seek to usurp the natural order of life either through the abuse of medical, scientific, chemical, electronic or political means tend to end up with a self-inflicted series of maladies.

To accord with the new age order a slimy breed of antagonist is spawned whose whole delight is to feed upon the carcasses of those disabled in the field of play by the just and honourable functioning of true men exerting their rightful authority.

These subnormal vermin infest the fringes of civilised life soliciting for custom amongst those that through the ignorance of pride have attempted to usurp the natural order of life and have received a bloody nose as a result.

But in the too precious fairyland lorded over by political pornocracies such natural consequences do not and cannot be numerically or statistically quantified and so cannot accord with their idea of a one world sanitised society in which any act that does not accord with their peculiar regime of enforced submission to the trivial and irrelevant truths of transient political expediency are regarded with such horror that the ownership of a plastic spoon and fork, if not cleared beforehand with the relevant authorities, is regarded as a potential act of terrorism.

Furthermore, those who tout for trade amongst those terrorised by synthetic cutlery wish always to appear as disinterested do-gooders and so they are forced to prostitute themselves and their honour by making vapid appeals to political doctrines of equality and religious ones of morality, neither of which they understand nor comprehend.

These culturally insignificant cowards delight in awarding grotesquely disproportionate awards to those hapless victims that need to be squeezed in their vices of jealous greed for like estate agents the more they can artificially inflate the value of their playmates' slums and the more they can make their victims squeal the greater the profits from their perverse practices.

Vast armies of people are now employed to ensure that we are all treated equally so long as some are far more financially equal than others. Accordingly obscene awards for trivialities are daily proclaimed so that the fat guzzling pigs standing in the trough are seen not only to defecate in it, but they also insist that our noses are rubbed in it as well. The reason for this is that there is a species of parasite that deal exclusively in what are known as relative truths and being only true by relativity they require the relative distances, numerical or otherwise, between themselves and others to be as great and obscenely disproportionate as possible.

However, the one thing that can be said of all relative truths is that they are rarely if ever true. Furthermore, being relative truths, they are inevitably subjective truths. Subjective or individual truths are, when compared to objective universal truths, always trivial and often irrelevant.

But some culturally decadent nations base the whole of their legislature upon subjective relative truths of a trivial and irrelevant nature. Thus, their courts overflow with intellectually subnormal law mongers introducing one irrelevancy after another concerning some trivial event that must permanently languish in some limbo of inadequate unidentifiable causes of no universal concern whatsoever.

They strut and pace around attempting to validate or justify a consequence to an inference when there is nothing to infer because the case has no cultural consequence other than to demonstrate that intelligence is limited and that stupidity isn't.

Legislative laws cannot and do not have precedence over cultural or natural law. This is because they deal exclusively in synthetic truths which are founded upon compounding subjective relative truths with contingent truths.

Thus, all legislative laws require relative that is subordinate clauses and thus all legislative laws are open to dispute and disrepute according to how well they are formulated or synthesised.

But such laws are inevitably formulated by those who are least qualified for the task. The more relative clauses they introduce the greater the ease with which anyone can avoid being brought to account.

Cultural laws however are not synthetic laws for man cannot synthesise that which is a priori that is before his intellect has been established.

Universal laws precede man just as do the square, the circle, the colours, the oceans and the stars.

The lives of intelligent men quickly become pointless and meaningless when statute, case and common laws conspire with decadent and diseased democracies to usurp the universal authoritative cultural laws of this planet and replace them with a plethora of inadequate prescriptive definitions of relative truths based upon their particular and peculiar interpretations of reality.

Without a strong cohesive creative culture, the individual has no friend, they have no hiding place, they possess no credibility they cannot apply for sanctuary.

They are alone – isolated threads of a destroyed fabric of universal brotherhood floating around aimlessly in an undefined space ever available to be sucked into that vast vacuum created when cultures die and are replaced by jealous greed and dictatorial democracies supported and paid for by their cronies in commerce.

When this occurs whole generations become apathetic and quickly develop a political and religious scepticism that leads towards an anomie so deep and pervasive that people turn to work or drugs to escape their lives of endless boredom.

Exactly! The globalisation of humanity can thus proceed unchecked and unabated. But as the one world super democracy and its henchmen in commerce plough their way through the lives of others, they espy other cultures who have escaped their mindless moronic meddling.

A jealous hatred of those who have the audacity to live a natural and ordered existence is followed by an obscene chauvinistic display of mindless patriotism that culminates in a vicious onslaught against that culture and that nation that had dared to ignore the postulates of culturally illegitimate and culturally illegal laws, acts and pronouncements.

Man was not created and put upon this planet to be abused or molested by gobby hags or vicious henchmen who are paid and empowered by diseased and degenerate political systems which use transient, irrelevant and trivial truths to justify their authority to inflict their intellectually deranged subjective realities upon the disarmed and disenfranchised in order that they can repeatedly profit from using and abusing others.

Such people have no interest in the quality of life – they are and become obsessed with quantities, the more nominal and notional the better for money only possesses power when it has very little if any nominal value whilst retaining a grossly inflated notional value.

Great cultures pay their members not in paper promises but in real estate and actualities founded upon absolute values generated by intellectual coherent constructs that regard all living creatures as of being of equal worth and thus equally worthy to share in the wealth that is common to all created beings.

But decadent cultures, societies and their political systems and their lapdogs in the state run brothels of law, order and commerce squander our inheritance by frittering away their abilities counting their fortunes arrived at by a persistent and pernicious adulation of those relative truths that the tyranny of greed and depravity have made into essential truths.

But these truths are only essential to them and are thus peculiar truths and thus universally irrelevant.

Societies that become enslaved by the tyranny of greed embark upon an exercise of attempting to justify the unjustifiable and when this fails, they simply cease to resist thus the more obscenely disproportionate their financial superiority the happier they become – or hope they become. But greed let loose without cultural boundaries or guidelines is a vicious and uncontrollable beast.

Once unrestrained by intellectual constructs it turns upon its guardians and drives them into an apathy and fear that torments their souls and forces them to adopt irrational draconian measures to avoid any possible threat to their financial superiority.

Thus, numbers become the justifying principle by and through which all things are measured. Thus, culture and life itself are thrown upon a barrow that is pushed into the faces of the culturally disinherited whilst the costermongers dream up new schemes of flooding their captive markets with culturally irrelevant trash and trivia that must be bought at such a cost to humanity and the environment.

Strong cohesive creative cultures deny others the right and authority to debase basic human freedoms by refusing to permit them to convert their irrelevant and trivial truths into categorically imperative constitutional laws that then attempt to weigh up and cost every intellectually universally valid constructive idea in terms of an arbitrary numerical relative sum of assumed value – this value being relative to a nation's assumed wealth in financial terms.

Thus, everything is put in terms of cost because costermongers, usurers and profiteers cannot think otherwise.

But creative cultures would and do create societies in which no person, corporation or organisation is able or capable of using their numerical wealth to disenfranchise, abuse, use, pollute or enslave others for their own profit.

Numerical wealth would become totally subordinated to cultural wealth. Money loses all power to persuade or corrupt when the basic necessities of life are granted as of right.

Every person who agrees to be bound by the codes of conduct necessary for their culture to remain fair and just would be granted free and unlimited access to those creative pursuits that are necessary to convert ideas and concepts into those useful and accessible forms that enrich the lives of all living organisms.

One method to make all members of a culture accountable to the whole world would be to issue everyone with a cultural credit card which would entitle members to the protection and benefits that their culture would and could afford them.

Such a card could be used to vote and could record how one voted. In creative cohesive cultures no secrecy is needed or necessary. One's individual choice is not some inappropriate and misunderstood casting of lots in some portacabin in the senile hope that chance will help one to decide between one preordained dysfunctional organisation rather than another and that this will somehow enrich one's culture, one's life, or that of planet earth and it has to be an honourable choice using open and honourable and truly democratic methods.

Corrupt political practices, their law enforcers and managers and their cronies in commerce pay themselves in direct proportion to how morally, ethically, culturally and intellectually dysfunctional and incapable they are or have become.

But this is because they have no cultural criteria by which to judge the degree of obscene selfishness that their actions display.

A cultural credit card would make such obscenities a thing of the past because no matter how much they paid themselves they could never buy that which they seek the most – cultural credibility. Their money would become worthless for they would be unable not only to buy their cultural credibility they would be unable to bribe it. They would possess no cultural freedom and thus would be unable to pollute this planet with their peculiarly diseased versions of ownership and control. The culture of a nation would be in control, commerce would not. Such cultural freaks would become that nightmare that stalks all selfish greed and they would become those lonely culturally isolated nobodies going nowhere other than the cash machine.

The rich tend to believe that not only are they numerically superior because they possess numerical wealth but that this somehow entitles them to possess 'culture' per se.

But culture has very little if anything to do with artefacts, music, paintings, books or the like for these things can be bought and sold.

Good, intelligent, skilful, meaningful or accessible intellectual constructs that is ideas expressed in a skilful and useful manner cannot be bought or sold for ideas are those precious concepts that form the basis of those ideals that are used to form the culture of a nation.

As non-material entities the cultural constructs of a nation deal exclusively in those areas of the mind of man and form the reason and purpose for his existence.

Those who use and abuse the natural universal cultural duties of justice and fairness to enrich themselves and their cronies at the expense of others generally do not understand this. However, they are usually acutely aware not only of the cultural dishonour they have brought upon themselves but that by being seen to have become cultural inadequates they rush off to the opera, the galleries, the tawdry and demeaning antique boutiques looking for and paying for that which they cannot possess and cannot deserve or cannot be entitled to.

But just as the rich cannot possess the unpossessable neither can the poor or miseducated. Needless to say, decadent societies fill the void in the souls of their slaves with a two-dimensional cartoon culture created by cardboard cut-out cultural inadequates that regurgitate the ineffectual trivial truths of modernism founded upon quantity and size.

Thus, a process that began a century ago has with the aid of technology spiralled out of control. If what is said or shown is meaningless – no matter.

Turn up the colour, turn up the volume, turn the handle faster, condense reality, churn out vast quantities, obliterate time, turn night into day, shout scream and bawl 24/7 – no time to stop, no time to think.

But some thoughts take days or weeks even years to develop into perfect projections of reality. Therefore, if what is hourly projected upon those lumps of glass that have become the crystal balls of popular culture were not politically sanitised or culturally censored then the ethereal mists that float before the eyes of the nation could condense and leave a clear and distinct image of how decadent and diseased we have all become.

Thus, the quantitative truths that are essential for diseased and decadent democracies to function in their pits of slime and secrecy must be proclaimed daily as being a true representation of reality. Size and numbers are all that matter. Accordingly, pornography is no danger to pornocracies and can be daily displayed. Violence and murder are no danger for such vicious assaults upon the value of life are what pornocracies encourage throughout this planet. Size matters no matter how hideous or dysfunctional. Accordingly those lumps of glass, those culturally inadequate crystal balls, undergo a form of plasmatic transmutation in order that the audience may receive digitised dictates direct from their dictators and the ectoplasm may be moulded and formed into a supple and compliant medium in order that the minute by minute bulletins regarding the success or failure of some irrelevant and trivial political drama may be displayed in all its pointless and meaningless perfection.

Thus, trash and trivia take pride of place upon those perfect plasmatic pictures that delight in displaying political ineptitude. Those cultures that base the value and worth of humans according to their relative size also delight in inflicting as much pain and suffering upon those at a distance so that the scale of their crimes and its subsequent minute fleeting pictorial representation are so dimensionally insignificant that the true dimensions of their crime against humanity is never revealed. Nevertheless, cultural crimes committed and hidden by distorted perspectives and slimy secrecy will count and will be counted against those who have colluded in their commitment and thus they will become cultural criminals. It is the job of universal cultures and their members to expose these cultural criminals and hold them to account. If anyone fails to act in defence of their culture, then they may be regarded as a cultural coward and thus lose all credibility and honour.

17 Creating a Culture

THE PURPOSE OF creating a new culture or joining an existing one is that by doing so if that culture is constructed using universally acceptable and applicable intellectually valid ideas that uphold the natural dignity and honour that the unique awareness of reality that living creatures possess and that unique awareness of themselves that man alone possesses then such a culture cannot be challenged or overthrown by transient political or religious systems. Furthermore, such a culture if founded upon the natural objective realities of existent life would possess the authority to establish codes of conduct by and through which the propriety of those actions taken by its members would be judged and regulated. Such a culture would have the moral and ethical authority to draw up and bind those cultural contacts that are essential not only to protect man's honour and the enormous emotional and physical effort and cost required to raise his offspring. Such a culture would also be required to educate them and to protect them from idle interference but also to protect itself from being brought into ridicule and disrepute.

Such cultures therefore have a moral and ethical duty to support and protect their members for the honour of a man is directly linked to the credibility of his culture. The degree to which a nation recognises and honours its obligations to its culture and to its menfolk is seen by other cultures as an indication of how civilised or perverted that nation has become.

Likewise, the females of a nation who freely choose to become women by making themselves relative to the culture of the menfolk of that nation must obey the cultural codes of conduct that is expected from them. Further if they forsake being femme solo and become women and further agree to become wives then they are duty bound to honour those cultural contracts necessary for any offspring to be brought up in a well-balanced environment.

If any culture allows itself to be brought into disrepute because it cannot or will not control the conduct of its members or its religious or political systems, then it becomes a degenerate one. If it wilfully persists in degenerating, then it becomes a decadent one.

Decadent cultures therefore do not possess any moral or ethical legitimacy and cannot enact universally applicable or acceptable laws. The laws of such cultures are universally illegal. Any universal acts of aggression whether by military, economic, political, scientific, chemical or technological means are illegitimate and illegal acts.

Being illegitimate and illegal acts, they are by definition acts of terrorism for lacking any moral or ethical validity they are employed solely to coerce others by and through fear.

Decadent cultures that remain wilfully ignorant of their universal cultural duties and responsibilities must be removed by true men exercising their truly democratic rights using a truly democratic system. If in the exercise of their truly democratic rights, they are forced to create new religious and political systems then so be it.

The hypothetical truths of science, the emotional and subjective truths of the individual, the transient contingent truths of politics, the inflexible self-justifying truths of computation, the true by definition alone truths of language, the repetitive platitudinous truths of religion, the synthetic retrospective truths of statute law, the irrelevant non-essential trivial truths of popular culture and the relative truths of societies cannot in themselves or when compounded together usurp, alter or compare with those unitary all-embracing universally acceptable and applicable objectively self-evident axiomatic truths that form the foundation upon which reason rests and provides the purpose for which life was intended.

Such truths are conceptualised and converted into cultures which grow through time into those essential and necessary intellectual constructs that alone possess the moral, religious, ethical and political authority to create, define and enforce those codes of conduct, cultural contracts and cultural laws that can generate those absolute truths that are required for the just and fair functioning of all those social systems that depend upon human beings acting in an honourable and dignified manner.

A nation can synthesise as many laws as it wishes yet they will always remain synthetic particular constructs whether they be common laws arising out of retrospection, statute laws from the legislature or case laws arising out of precedence. All synthetic laws arise out of particular events that are particular to a time and place, are particular to a people and their environment, they are specific to their political systems and most importantly they are particular to their degree of civilisation.

Synthetic laws are therefore peculiar laws and thus cannot be universal laws. Peculiar laws that are proper to and for a particular people cannot be universalised and therefore cannot be used to judge the validity or the propriety or the legality of those actions taken by other nations.

Accordingly the law mongers of one nation cannot pronounce upon the actions of another thus all unilateral declarations of intent to interfere in the affairs of other cultures and all unilateral acts of aggression can only be judged against those universal standards of behaviour and conduct that the independence of time and the objective authority of the world's cultural heritage have constructed and made available as a criteria by which such unilateral actions can and must be judged.

Accordingly, those political embarrassments that would have us believe that they possess some antecedent peculiar right to pontificate upon matters of universal importance are simply over-inflated balloons of cultural insignificance kept afloat by their own perpetual political flatulence.

If challenged to account for their actions they call upon their law officers to justify the unjustifiable. But these brazen tarts are ever keen to prostitute their honour and intellectual integrity because they belong to a profession that survives by adopting a sycophantic obsequious reverence for anything that might solicit them peculiarly disproportionate pecuniary profits and all the illegitimate honours of rank that debased humanity can offer.

As in all pornocracies universal truths are subpoenaed to appear before their sick and diseased democracies where behind closed doors they are tortured and mutilated until they reflect and accord with what their culturally corrupt captors have decided to be the case.

No matter what is said or done universal truths are eternally recurring independently arrived at intellectual constructs that transcend time and all possible or conceivable material existences.

If there is a creator, then all that can truly be said of them is that they are 'the truth'.

If God is the truth, then creation is his truth. God therefore may be love, he may be great, he may be the totality of all possible worlds but the one thing he cannot be is a totality of lies.

No lie can inhere in any creator, and no creator can tolerate a single falsehood thus the more one lies and cheats the further from the truth one becomes.

Just as truth is composed of varying aspects of different and differing meanings and degrees of relativity and importance so to do lies have a structure that can dictate when that point of transition between idle inaccuracy and falsehoods has been reached.

One may claim that a dog or horse or any animal is a sacred and beautiful creature that excels man in many respects. But no animal has been created for our purpose and thus no animal has been granted our intellectual awareness and thus no animal, apart from humans, can lie. The purpose therefore of creating culture is so that men can function as human beings rather than wild irrational animals.

Decadent and sick nations that have destroyed their cultures taunt and bait their menfolk hoping to provoke them to lash out wildly at those miserable squirts who attempt to dominate and destroy the sanctity of the individual by persistent irrational acts of self-interested greed and perversion.

But if one did retaliate, one would then automatically lose, for retaliation is what all bullies and cowards desire the most when they feel secure and entrenched in their pits and bunkers. Retaliation gives them a handle, or name by which to hold you down and inflict yet more mindless acts of vandalism against you and your beliefs.

The natural laws of creation inhere in the individual and if any individual is subjected to the wild irrational behaviour of others, then it is the cultural duty of all other living creatures to come to their assistance.

The natural laws of creation are absolute laws which cannot be denied or overturned by the peculiar synthetic laws of particular nations.

The truth and purpose of existence belongs with and in every living creature, but it is only man that can truly be fully aware of what that purpose is.

To move away from or to be wilfully ignorant of what that purpose is, is to lie outside civilised life. To persist in denying those universal truths that make every living creature of equal worth and to deny them the right to act as free agents is to act against created life. The purpose of culture is to enact, construct and create laws that deny those who act against created life any part in the process of unifying and civilising creation into one great chain of truth.

The ultimate aim of all cultures would be to coalesce into one universal culture of justice and fairness so as to enable one truth to arise out of mankind.

This one truth is that which all prophets and sons of God die for and thus it is what all men have been created to die for.

The days when kings led their armies into battle are long gone. When bravery and courtesy ruled a potentate gladly accepted a challenge to settle disputes one man against one man so that others could be spared.

But since a disastrous series of pathetically impotent potentates caused the demise of that honourable order of personal accountability and liability the west has sunk into its own shame of infamy. Hiding behind the skirts of women and religion they destroyed all forms of sanctuary and denied the universal authority of a nation's cultural heritage to bind and protect its citizens from the machinations of the state.

Accordingly, from that point in time all living creatures ceased to represent the creative truth of a benign universal spirit and became the public property of debauched supremists.

People could then be legally bought and sold, animals could be wilfully tortured and mutilated for pleasure and profit. Culture itself became materialised objects that only the elitist cultural criminals could afford.

Vast armadas could be deployed to conduct indiscriminate acts of terrorism against any target because all life was now publicly accountable for the actions of the maniacs who had enslaved them and so insane amounts of weaponry could be unleashed against anyone anywhere so long as those who ordered the button to be pushed or the lever to be pulled were at the maximum relative numerical distance from their illegal and illegitimate acts.

But no individual living creature can ever be regarded as public property and no individual living creature can ever be regarded as private property.

All living creatures are therefore the property of that culture to which they belong, but they only belong if they agree to be bound by its laws and its codes of conduct.

Man is no ordinary animal, he is no political or religious pawn, he is no madman's toy or target – he is a cultural asset.

Without men cultures grow weak – without true men they shrivel up and die.

When cultures shrivel up and die then so do civilisations and when civilisations die then so does the truth and when the truth dies then so does our creator.

18 The Final Story

As THE MONOFORM of modernism proclaims its one world theory its already degraded democracies degenerate further into pornocratic monocracies which extol the virtues of a free market mismanagement that elevates their worthless cultural credibility to new heights of insignificance by redefining human values in terms not of honour, truth, trust or decency but in notional numerical values of currencies that require the support of vast arsenals of indiscriminately destructive weaponry and an army of dysfunctional and miseducated henchmen to enforce their morally bankrupt beliefs.

These currencies which are supported by a promise to bash anyone up who doesn't subscribe to their persuasive power to pollute and destroy the lives and freedoms of others have, in themselves, no value whatsoever.

Their value consists of paper promises that are formulated using debased languages and cultures founded upon elitism and pride of possessions.

Thus, anyone who subscribes to such currencies are given and are promised the freedom to use and abuse others in return for them being advocates and supporters of the elitist dream of living in that exclusivity and privacy that excludes anyone who does not subscribe to their 'pig in the trough' world.

Such divisive and morally dysfunctional democracies and those pornocratic monocracies that they will eventually become must be replaced before a one world leader emerges from the ruins of civilisation to proclaim that an ultimate theoretical and hypothetical relationship has been achieved between the world's political, religious, economic and military leaders that empowers them to declare that the world now possesses only one valid unit of currency, only one valid political system, only one scientific road to freedom, only one type of economy and only one super state in which reality and language means whatever it is stated to mean on any particular day.

Let us call a mixture of power to, through and by a culturally stable and culturally advanced and aware people a cultural 'centocracy'. But in a world that controls the meaning and construction of words a word that has to be invented such as 'centocracy' which refers to an intellectually viable and understandable concept that promotes the idea of reuniting the now various and diverse isolated and separated ideas that once formed the seedlings of a universal culture and reforming them into a coherent political movement that would establish a national movement for cultural, political, religious and commercial accountability, such a word would be unacceptable because, by law, only minorities are now permitted to create their own culture and only minorities are now permitted to create their own language.

When one considers that the west, despite the technological revolutions of the past few decades, still insist on using outdated, outmoded, logically illogical, non-representative, monopolistic, intellectually senile forms of voting and further restrict these demonstrations of people power to seedy municipal buildings without even having the decency to call a paid national holiday then this form of democratic disrespect needs to be replaced. A true culture can never arise nor can a true democracy if political systems insist on using a single strand of logic to justify the election of those choices made by elitists to perpetuate their peculiar political systems.

Their one cross, one thumbprint type of voting was introduced because the 'us' – the religious and financial supremists – did not really want the 'them' – the illiterate rabble – to be seen, let alone heard, thus a mono-form of universal suffrage was introduced that has proved indispensable in keeping the elite exclusive and their cronies in commerce safe from public accountability.

If the universal cultural laws of a nation reside within the intellect of man, then his intellect must be granted the freedom to fully express itself.

As politicians never reach their bribe by dates there is an urgent need to replace them with direct cultural mandates from the people. The choices made by the people need not be secret and should not be made in secret for this separation between belief and choice was only thought necessary to stop the local barons and their thugs from knocking down your hovel and eating your chickens if you failed to vote for them.

But as then as now new democracies that haven't had the time to degen-erate become accountable to the bully barons and if these new democracies fail to fit in with what the political perverts state has to be the case, they allow homes to be demolished and land to be stolen.

If there is to be only one world then it must be a cultural one. If there is to be only one political system, then it must be a true one. If there is to be an end to sectarianism, then there has to be a new religion. If there is to be an end to hate and fear, then there must be an end to that chauvinistic military pride that comes from coward power and if there is to be an end to greed then there must be an end to individualism and isolationism.

The elitist one world isolationists who have abused their democratic freedoms to establish pornocratic monocracies are forced to use their military might and firepower to support their worthless currencies and their meaningless cultures for being isolated from humanity itself makes them culturally insignificant and thus morally ineffectual and thus only fit to be universally ignored.

Being acutely aware of their universal insignificance they are thus forced to abuse their supremacy by employing culturally illegal and illegitimate financial and military force to coerce others to prostitute their integrity and honour in the hope that this will degrade and ultimately destroy those cultures that ignore or resist that mindless drivel that persistently drips from the lips of all dictatorial dysfunctional democracies.

Having indulged in disreputable, dishonest and dishonourable acts of financial and military aggression since their foundation such nations must enact peculiar and pernicious laws in an attempt to justify their inhuman acts of self-interested interference in the lives and cultures of others.

If they fool themselves into believing that they have succeeded in establishing a culturally legitimate nation, then those illegitimate acts that created such a structure become enshrined in their replacement cultures and thus those replica cultures demand and expect a repetitious replay of those distorted renditions of reality wherein their original dishonesty and mindless violence are reformed into heroic acts of self-determination. Accordingly, very few books, magazines, videos or films now exist in which a death by gunfire is not accompanied by powerful pornographic visions of perfectly polished people indulging their individual fantasies and if it is to have cultural significance it should include some interstellar or stratospheric release of rockets, death rays or guided missiles directed at digitally dehumanised creatures on their way to the local shops. This form of intellectual terrorism is essential in order that the offspring of such cultures come to believe that they must belong to this gun toting self-indulgent gang and thus a pornographic stratocracy develops whose purpose is to compile strategies by and through which armaments industries can force their intellectually inadequate and morally feeble leaders into prostituting their humanity by permitting and encouraging their allies and cronies in commerce to bankroll their latest illogical insult to logic and democracy when they ask their electorate yet again to say 'yes' to what their cartoon cultures tell them is the next step on the road to nowhere.

But this road to nowhere, some forgotten pit of cultural and moral isolation becomes an intellectual no man's land in which inadequate and dishonest representations of reality are compounded with debased and decadent languages by and through which all words can now, by inference, refer to some act of moral or sexual degeneracy.

Thus, no matter what is said it must, to accord with the new age ordering of everybody about, be able to be distorted to fit the beliefs of others whose beliefs have been distorted by that misinformation and miseducation that is necessary to support decadent democracies. Diseased democracies require the support of large numbers of misinformed, miseducated and dysfunctional voters who must be granted the right to be as greedy and selfish as possible, who need to possess an elitist sense of worth and value, who are required to be indoctrinated in deformed and illogical belief systems regarding ownership and possession and who are encouraged to subscribe to others the same debased and distorted intentions that they harbour themselves.

They must possess no cultural criteria by which to judge their own actions for they thus come to believe that all humanity is as naturally debased and perverted as themselves. Accordingly gross acts of injustice are thus justified because anyone who does not bow down to the golden calf of capitalism, consumerism and culturally illegitimate and morally decadent democratic systems must by default be guilty of some offence, the exact nature of which exists in that it's possible so it's probable so it must be likely hypothetical land of the intellectually inadequate.

Whole nations and whole groups of people can and do become branded with illogical and improper epithets whose reality, though mythical, is encouraged by the warmongers and the financial and religious and political supremists who insist on using historical misinformation to prove that the divisions to be found upon this planet have arisen through and by some god given antecedent right for the fortunate to segregate humanity into sectarian factions.

But the divisions to be found upon this planet are the result of greed and stupidity – the greatest enemies to cultural cohesion and quality of life. Dishonest and decadent political systems when combined with that sectarian bigotry that religions encourage proclaim that every individual has the right to possess more than it is right to possess.

Not only do they proclaim that every individual has a right to possess more than it is right to possess they also state that they have a right to possess without any cultural controls over their possessions. Thus, everyone can not only legitimately use and abuse other living creatures they can use and abuse their surplus possessions and are thus politically freed to indulge in obscene displays of profligacy and wastage.

Without any cultural controls over ownership and consumption whole nations become as fat headed, greedy, arrogant, self-interested and as dangerously stupid as their citizens.

If such nations then embark upon an insane quest to establish a one-world super-democracy, then all those acts of gross injustice that will be required to force others to submit will be validated using the process of democratisation to justify any means to that end.

But processes cannot be used to justify themselves or they become self-relative, self-validating, self-satisfying systems which revolve around a single self-centred and centring idea.

Mathematics cannot function or work without being composed of numbers that automatically refer to other numbers and thus to themselves. Worse still the results of any computation can only be validated and justified by reference to another set of numbers which because they now form the basis by and through which all things are measured must be significant even if in themselves, they have no reality and signify only that which others wish us to believe.

Languages cannot be used to justify themselves because they are fragile elastic structures that are easily deformed and fractured. Furthermore, they cannot be made self-referential without becoming irrational. For instance, if one was to write, 'This sentence does not contain seven words' then the words and meaning become confused. One cannot make a language self-referential unless one is lying or trying to justify a process using the process itself which is stupid.

Political systems cannot be used to justify themselves because political processes depend entirely upon the self-justifying process of mathematics and the deformation of language.

Religious systems cannot be used to justify themselves because they are entirely based upon peculiar and particular beliefs which are incompatible with other beliefs because to be particular means, to them, to be especially selected – to be set apart from and not just "a" part of one whole unified structure.

The laws of a nation cannot be used to justify themselves because they are even more particular and peculiar to a time, place and people than religions. Most laws are simply the absurd manifestations of that fear of loss, and need for greed that surrounds and encumbers people and forces them to live as cowardly subservient drones because people actually believe that laws reside in some mythical and mysterious heaven whereas in reality, they reside in themselves and their cultures.

Cultures, however, are and cannot be self-referential and are not bound by particular beliefs. They are composed of intellectual constructs that use every type of process and take one process and compare its functioning with another process. They take particular beliefs and make them relative to universal and objective beliefs. They take analytic truths and compare them to transient, synthetic truths. They take sound and light; they take ideas and emotions and combine them into usable and accessible forms. They are the manifestation of that four-dimensional universe that resides within the intellect of man. They are above the political and religious dogmas that infest this planet.

The self-interested bigotry and dogmatization that is endemic to transient, political systems that employ a miseducated and dysfunctional electorate to rubber stamp intellectually inadequate propositions debars people who support and subscribe to such systems from having the ethical or moral authority to make universally relevant or culturally binding declarations.

It is only the culture of a nation that could possess any universally acceptable right to make declarations of intent.

Western democracies that employ a monopolistic logic and an intellectually senile form of suffrage cannot be considered a competent or legitimate source of or for moral authority.

The job of all men is to become true men by becoming culturally aware and active.

The cultural wastelands created by decadent and debased political and religious systems can only be made virile and fertile again by granting inalienable rights to all men as these would enable them to act as caretakers to their culture.

The young of a nation must be educated in their cultural duties and granted those absolute rights that will enable them to live free from those debts imposed upon them by those parasitic, political, financial and religious usurers that infest all those nations which have adopted degenerate and dysfunctional democratic systems of governance.

Cultures naturally heal themselves when intellectually inadequate, parasitic maggots are removed from the lives of living creatures. But parasitic maggots cling to their positions of control and power using military and financial terrorism and can only be removed by a campaign of cultural awareness that empowers people to demand their cultural birthright to have their nation controlled using a comprehensive form of voting.

Depraved political systems that depend upon and insist upon using the most stupid, outdated and breathtakingly inadequate forms of voting must be replaced by using a comprehensive voting form that not only reflects the intellectual creativity endemic to men, but which bypasses those self-appointed cultural cowards that pass for our elected representatives.

One cannot reason with stupidity. One cannot reason with greed, and one cannot reason with the religious bigot. Western democracies are designed to stop intelligent rational creatures from deciding how their own nations should be run and organised.

They accomplish this by refusing to grant their citizens any absolute rights and they refuse to adopt comprehensive and far-reaching methods by and through which the individual can fully express their cultural and political views. To add insult to injury they also refuse to grant unconditional sanctuary to their electorate in order that no one can hide or avoid the state sponsored and controlled financial, intellectual and social terrorism which they use to control not only their own nationals but as there is now to them only one world, they extend this franchise to include any individual anywhere that is foolish enough to subscribe to their one world democratically enhanced super slavery system.

It is culturally competent and aware people who decide what their towns and cities should be and what they should look like – not politicians or commerce. It is the culture of a nation that should control how the kitty is divided, and it is the culture of a nation that provides its people with the facts and figures as to who is buying what, who is making what and for what reason. Most importantly it is the culture of a people that reveals who is paying for and supporting intellectual, sexual, political, economic, religious, environmental and military terrorism. No secrecy is required in culturally cohesive societies for there cannot be anything anywhere to hide. But as stated language becomes self-referential and thus absurd and illogical when one attempts to use it to justify the unjustifiable.

Fear leads to terror when people lack control over their own lives and when they become powerless to protect those that are daily murdered and slaughtered in the name of some degenerate perverted antiquated and senile form of democracy that has as much ethical and moral authority and justification to act the way it does as did the elitist lunatics who first thought up the idea of political, economic and military supremacy as being the only way forward.

There is no greater terror than to watch helplessly as the innocent are targeted by those cultural cowards who hide behind illogical and defective political and religious systems that have been cobbled together out of that jealousy and greed that always accompanies the intellectually and emotionally inadequate and who use remote control systems to destroy their supposed, imaginary or invented enemies. But they become the enemy themselves because they are beyond any cultural control systems and thus are evil. Evil means ill in the head and stupid people who are ill in the head can do as they please for those cultural constraints and those cultural contracts that formerly bound and restrained them have been cut and severed by self-interested greed and a hatred of all that might restrict its vicious campaign for world domination.

Each person who reads this book needs only to lift their pen and write out how their future and that of all other living creatures can be changed if they are willing to communicate with their culture in a positive and meaningful way. If each person who reads this book educates themselves to that degree of competence and awareness that is required to make well balanced and appropriate decisions and if they are willing to discover what is true in itself and not just what they are told or believe to be true, then the first steps will have been taken in returning life to its original purpose.

Furthermore, if they are willing to create a culture founded upon justice and fairness and if they are willing to share their ideas, their wealth, their time and their hopes with all other living creatures then their culture will become a universally applicable one.

It is only universally applicable cultures that possess the necessary moral, ethical and intellectual authority to grant people those things that are essential to ensure a good quality of life, for only universally applicable cultures are true in themselves.

Truth is what is real and reality depends upon how things are presented to us.

Only universal cultures founded upon objective intellectual constructs that define justice and fairness can be true for they are the intellectual manifestations of those everlasting and eternal truths that existed before time and space began, that were there before man was first thought of and which existed before any god or creator could exist for without the truth no world, no life and no worthwhile existence is truly possible.

19 State Sponsored Stupidity – Eternal & Unlimited

THE CREATIVITY OF man is an ongoing daily process.

Given the duty to procreate, as well as being intellectually active and emotionally stable, the cultures that he is responsible for establishing, nurturing, enlarging and making available to others enables him to achieve an honourable status that sets him apart from all other living creatures.

Needless to state envy, jealousy, greed and stupidity all conspire to worm their way into such stable and coherent structures in order that they themselves may profit from the functioning of true men who being rational well-balanced creatures freely give what they can in order that their culture may grow and prosper.

Natural healthy cultures ensure that all of their members grow and advance together and thus such cultures are governed and regulated to ensure that no single or group of organisms advance at the expense and disadvantage of others.

Corrupt and diseased cultures spawn large numbers of deformed and gangrenous specimens that possess no internal or external control mechanisms and thus such abnormal growths are free to run amok, their cancerous expansion causing them to mutate into parasitic entities that ultimately destroy those upon which they feed.

Universally creative, stable and constant cultures therefore require strong and effective defence mechanisms to ensure that they remain immune to those forces that promote the destruction and destitution of the many for the benefit of those who through a hatred of their own inadequacies attempt to perpetually torment and enslave others for their own entertainment or profit.

When cultures are weakened by religious or political interference there is a danger that the few, who by employing that mindless violence that one associates with the intellectually challenged, are able to elevate themselves into positions of influence and power from which they mesmerise the many into believing that this is how it should be.

The many, seeing only privilege and exclusivity resulting from depriving others of their fair share, seek to emulate and copy their self-appointed superiors and are thus contaminated with the same cancerous concepts that blind their senses and thus they cannot smell that foul stench that arises from themselves as they rot away in cultural insignificance in their prestigious and exclusive ghettos to greed.

Those who refuse to acknowledge the ethical legitimacy of such regimes are left behind to fester in some inconsequential political and financial limbo from which they are forced to watch their planet being tortured and mutilated, pressurised and squeezed into yielding all its stores and treasures to finance the security and privacy of the parasitic elite lest those that they daily defile seek to halt the rot.

Accordingly, the elite now require vast armour-plated vehicles to transport them to their exclusive developments from which they can tune in to watch their sick and deformed societies tear not only themselves apart but also witness those other nations and cultures which they have infected being ripped to shreds.

Having satisfied themselves that they are indeed fortunate and well off to be such supreme beings they can switch to watching their nations cultural highlights of one monkey screaming at or poking sticks at another in the state sponsored big brother asylum.

But stupidity, incompetence, greed, privacy and exclusivity are expensive perversions and when the state run, state sponsored asylum gets strapped for cash and the daily slaughter of the unborn creates chasms in the property market vast numbers of aliens need to be imported to decorate and fill those loathsome and noxious dwellings that have become so essential to and for the parasitic elite.

Fearing that the culturally, politically, socially and financially dispossessed might grumble too loudly and that these murmurings of discontent might be heard and understood by their new neighbours, culturally degenerate nations are forced to make proclamation after proclamation as to how everyone must, by law, sing along together to the same tune using the same lyrics.

This is thought to be essential, for if just one person were heard to sing out of tune or, worse still, sang their own lyrics, then some of these imported aliens might be offended and leave.

Needless to say all new arrivals are permitted to sing their own songs, no matter how badly and no matter how offensively because people in those sick societies that require and need these new people possess no rights and therefore many, having nowhere else to go, are forced to listen, for they themselves are in fact state owned and state controlled landless peasants that are at the mercy of unstable democratic dictatorships who can and do order them about and tell them what to do and what to think.

All democratic dictatorships possess the power to permit their imports carte blanche in usurping the cultural rights of others because the whole point of a deformed democracy is to destroy any connection between truth and reality and to destroy any cultural safeguards that might inhibit the quest for a one world super democracy.

Furthermore, when degenerate democracies succeed in destroying the link between truth and reality, they then feel free to pay their political and economic prisoners with paper promises that only promise to declare such agreements worthless and void when the time comes for the state to honour their word and pay up. Their political allies and cronies in commerce however are permitted to pay themselves disproportionately obscene amounts of paper promises with which they buy up all the essentials of life and then declare themselves bankrupt in order that their workers and slaves lose everything and have to start again.

Thus, the many are condemned to slave a lifetime for a few lumps of tin and plasterboard whilst singing along with their neighbours lest the walls of their culturally sterile hovels vibrate to a different tune.

Meanwhile those political and religious contagionists that have empowered themselves to control every aspect of their meaningless lives become so debauched and pornocratic by their own inability to know what is right and proper that they encourage their captives to freely indulge in all forms of degrading behaviour.

Such deranged systems of governing the lives of others are ever keen to profit from the misery they cause in others and when those lonely specimens of manhood, finding themselves culturally isolated, attempt to find some fleeting solace and refuge in the arms of some self-seeking hag, a purple fury of hypocritical indignation arises in their deformed minds that some of their slaves and captors are enjoying themselves at their expense.

Accordingly, some form of taxation must be imposed upon such pursuits and if this proves impracticable then those that perpetrate such acts must be criminalised for the beady eye of state sponsored greed is blinded by a jealous hatred of any activity that can generate both pleasure and profit and appears beyond their grasp.

Those self-seeking deformed specimens of womanhood who ply their trade amongst the weak and vulnerable must be elevated to the ranks of the oppressed in order that the parasitic elite may justify their exorbitant need to interfere with and control every aspect of life.

In the topsy-turvy world of the deranged and demented democrat however, those that ensnare and entrap others for profit must be seen and be portrayed as vulnerable victims of enigmatic forces, for all those that would profit from the necessities of life are the darlings of the free market economy and thus no matter how loathsome or despicable the trade then if money is involved then those that make it must be protected and thus controlled. If they cannot be controlled, then they must be outlawed and persecuted.

The problem that arises with such a system is that if some wish to feed and live upon the misery and degradation of others they need to create societies so unbalanced and so unfair that their members become so stressed out that they degenerate into mindless drudges who willingly give up control of their own lives and thus become victims of their own device who can then be lawfully and wilfully victimised.

The elite cannot therefore grant their inferiors with any absolute rights for to do so would force the elite to honour their pledges and promises. As all elitist parasitic regimes depend upon forcing people to acquiesce to their reforms and demands through political, financial, cultural, religious and economic terrorism then no true democracies can arise because all choices made by the people who live under elitist regimes are made under that duress and that fear that always arises in those who have no control over their own lives.

Such people cannot be said to be truly free for not only do they not possess any real control over their own lives, they possess no real control over their environment. Worse still they can only choose between a 'one world and it belongs to whoever can afford it' existence an 'us' or 'nothing' world in which the idea of two or more political, religious or cultural choices being made available for everyone to choose from cannot be allowed because some misguided and obviously unwell examples of the human race might just decide to opt out of the state sponsored asylum and create a culture and lifestyle that was beyond the control of the one world theorists.

In the one world super democracy that is fast becoming a reality you will not be permitted any freedom of choice because such choices, by definition, have already been made for you and were made before you even existed. This all or nothing world is the fundamental principle upon which all deformed democracies are based.

However, to give the appearance of unlimited choice sick and diseased democracies and the sick and diseased cultures that they engender must interfere with and attempt to destroy all forms of honourable conduct by declaring that those cultural contracts freely entered into by others must now be made subordinate to and made relative to whichever political or religious system has been adopted by the elite to govern and control the lives of others.

Decadent democracies therefore delight in seeing people marrying their horse or coal-bunker and think it eminently suitable for people of the same gender to bring up and educate the innocent and the impressionable for by allowing such unnatural choices and by allowing such unbalanced upbringing the chances of any children growing up into well-balanced individuals capable of joining or creating well balanced cultures becomes that much more remote.

This belief in free choice and its numerical implications is an essential feature of all demented democracies for it implies the freedom to make stupid choices and it implies that freedom necessary for others to allow life itself to be constrained and restrained, interfered with and controlled, to be modified and mutilated.

Accordingly, no matter how bizarre or ridiculous, no matter how obscene or degrading, no matter how vile or contemptuous if the concept or course of action chosen is chosen by the majority of those mindless morons who thought up the absurdity in the first instance, then such people come to believe in their own peculiar versions of reality.

If life itself then becomes endangered by the indiscriminate use and adaptation of principles founded upon inadequate and distorted renditions of reality which are then justified by an illogical belief in the power of numbers to make the absurd rational then the real world will quickly degenerate into a frightfully unjust and fearful place filled with dishonourable self-seeking political and religious bigots who hide their cultural inadequacies using that slimy secrecy necessary to justify their use of financial and military force to dispossess others of their natural born freedoms and expectations.

It is, therefore, the job of all true men to create, support and defend cultures that make those political and religious cultural inadequates a thing of the past. The strong cohesive all-inclusive cultures that true men are duty bound to create in order to protect life itself from being interfered with and by non-essential surplus to requirements intellectually subnormal self-seeking maggots will then be free to truly reflect the creative intelligence and capacity of mankind to heal itself and thus once mankind has proven itself capable of curing those festering wounds caused by incompetence, greed and stupidity, it can function as originally intended.

Unfortunately, those political and religious embarrassments that currently control our lives are too keenly aware of their own tenuous grip upon and claim for support from their victims.

A vast array of illegitimate cultural reforms is required to keep the privileged. To keep them in this world of unreality a cartoon culture must be created in which anything is possible and if possible by implication it must be probable because those imitations of reality as propounded by their decadent replacement cultures as used in the west have adopted the concept of quantity over quality, thus spawning a whole philosophical system in which size, numbers and all forms of statistical evidence is how reality is to be classified and defined.

Thus, a world is created that is defined and classified by a numerical interpretation of value and worth coupled to a system of logic that confuses the probable and the possible and that states quantity of life is more important than quality of life.

Any acts therefore no matter how innocuous, no matter how inoffensive, if they are undertaken by true men as they attempt to improve the quality of their lives are treated with that shock and outrage that one associates with those that govern by and through that usurped and illegitimate authority that depends upon depriving others of their right to exist as free and independent self-governing entities.

So called advanced and civilised nations fearing that what they inflict upon their citizens and upon others might be practised upon themselves employ excessive numbers of slimy antagonists who creep around ever keen to inform upon and profit from the natural functioning of true men as they attempt to create a new culture in which all are not only equal, but in which all are welcome.

Such antagonists are hired by the state to interfere in all aspects of life but now especially in the domestic side of life, for the state well knows that to control its natural born enemies it must rigidly control houses and homes and deprive true men any outright control, or ownership, of either.

As part of this onslaught against any possibility of a culture arising to challenge their positions of power, elitist regimes and those deformations of democratic principles that they adopt must ensure that true men do not possess those absolute freedoms that are essential for them to function correctly. As a result, the commonplace and the trivial are criminalised and the normal and natural behaviour of the virile and active is elevated into life threatening situations.

Everything that a man would naturally do or say is now a criminal offence because it might upset one of the thousands of sects and divisions that now exist in those fragmented and unstable social structures as a result of that political or religious interference with those civilised cultures that naturally arise when human beings are left in that peace and tranquillity necessary for them to function properly.

Accordingly, all those necessary and natural expressions of misery and frustration that men are prone to are, in deformed and fractionalized cultures, are seen to be a threat, whereas in strong, well balanced cohesive cultures they are understood and catered for and form the driving force necessary for that culture to advance and remain strong and equitable.

In nations that have no real cultural values and that refuse to construct and publish meaningful bills of cultural rights, if such nations are led by culturally retarded party propagandists who ponce around gibbering on and on about how essential they are to life and the feeble and sick societies that they create then the elite of such societies will encourage and pay large numbers of malevolent sycophants to enforce their paymasters peculiarly vicious form of perverted justice by encouraging them to ensure that families and homes are torn apart by creating absurd distortions of a truth that artificially inflates the expectations of people and that forces them to live in a state controlled environment from which they cannot escape and then to subject them to those political and economic unrealities and pressures that the incompetence of greed combined with stupidity produces.

Life then becomes merely a struggle to survive from one meaningless and empty day to the next, thus causing a resentment and hatred to arise in the hearts of those so abused and thus they turn upon each other in that sickening dance to the death of those once fruitful and loving relationships that instead of growing and maturing into stable and culturally beneficial entities disintegrate and leave a sufficiency of rotting carcases and diseased minds for the parasitic elite and their cronies to feast upon.

Having presided over the collapse of their nation's culture and its codes of conduct and cultural contracts and having witnessed the misery and hardship that they are able to force their state owned and controlled serfs and slaves to endure the elite then award themselves offensively disproportionate awards, these awards now appearing mandatory for all those who deal with the remnants of those fledgling cultures that their greed and stupidity have caused to decay and disintegrate.

Yet such maggots have the insolence to argue that their excessive demands are justified for how else are they to be able to afford to live in that privacy and exclusivity that keeps them as secure and remote from their cultural crimes as possible.

The laws of nations that wish to live from the proceeds of immoral cultural reforms are formulated to prescribe a diet of division and deprivation in order that a zombified and dysfunctional electorate will emerge to form a reliable reservoir of ill-informed state controlled polling station fodder that will rubber stamp their latest insult to man's collective intelligence when they are asked to once again agree with yet more divisive laws that the elite state are urgently needed to safeguard one of this planet's demented democracies from being threatened by sensible, rational and justified ideas on how to change this world so that it represents our creative abilities and not our collective stupidity.

When demented democracies realise that they are seen for what they are, the sum total of mankind's inability to function correctly, they automatically default to a failsafe mode which promises health and wealth to all those who will disregard those values that make life worthwhile and meaningful and promise death and destruction to all else.

Their supporters and advocates unable and unwilling to conduct themselves in a creative and civilised manner by discussing issues using their intelligence and skill become the world's true terrorists for such democracies being painfully aware of their own tenuous grasp upon legitimacy and reality resort to that mindless and indiscriminate violence that they have employed throughout their history to get their own way.

Stung into action by their own political and moral inadequacies they rampage through this planet seeking out those that disagree with their deranged fantasies of a one world super state run, owned, funded and protected by perverted democratic principles and having found others unwilling to bow down to their symbols to greed and gluttony they dispossess them of their cultural rights and heritage and immediately import their own sickly and weedy cartoon cultures funded and supported by consumer based drivel as to how happy we all are in the west.

This denial of others possessing the legitimacy to create their own political systems, lifestyles, environments and cultures turns such mindlessly interfering nations into the world's true terrorists for such nations, hiding behind meaningless words such as 'modern democracy' become transfixed by the influence and power that their mindless dictators can use to deny others their human rights.

Entrenched in their blast proof bunkers they can, by remote control, force others to live without a true bill of rights, without a culture, without the absolute right to food, shelter and warmth and without the right to freely choose between a political and non-political world.

Thus, if an individual wishes to live within a culture that denies others the right to use deranged and demented distortions of a badly designed and illogical political system to create a set of peculiarly unbalanced and divisive laws the very purpose of which are to uphold and support the system that creates them, then this is a human right that cannot be denied.

The only way therefore that deranged democracies can enforce their peculiarly inefficient and culturally incompetent laws is by and through force of arms and economic sanctions which means either flying around indiscriminately bombing and shooting at anything that moves or flying around and indiscriminately polluting, destroying, impounding or spraying anything that doesn't move – just in case it can be eaten or used to mend those broken by the bombing.

20 Culture: Your Only True Friend

CULTURE, MEANING TO grow together towards a common goal, and thus sharing a common purpose, is the means by and through which the individual self becomes a real entity; a total and absolute object that cannot be molested or interfered with by other exterior organisms without those that do so being devalued and regarded as belonging to a class of evil and malicious subnormals that need to be controlled and modified and ultimately restructured into useful and worthwhile objects.

Those objects that possess the physical and intellectual integrity to function as independent living organisms that have an awareness of themselves can if they make this awareness relative to those universally acceptable set of ideals and concepts that form the basis of all legitimate cultures, these objects can never be isolated or lonely for by making themselves relative to and members of intellectually stable and coherent systems that possess an absolutely clear and distinct identity then those individuals that choose such cultures become absolute objective realities in themselves. As such they no longer exist as individually separated links of one vast chain that represents the creative ability of mankind and its creator, they become inexorably linked to all other living creatures irrespective of those creatures' awareness of themselves.

When individuals decide to link themselves to a set of concepts and ideals that are enforced to ensure a quality of life for all and not just for a few then they accept that, as civilised living entities, they must conduct themselves in a manner that permits them to act both as 'a part' and yet 'apart' from those wild irrational and often vicious type of animal to which their bodies belong.

When the self becomes an integral part of creation by accepting to be bound by those codes of conduct that govern the behaviour to be expected of that individual self and when that individual self agrees to accept those limitations to their desire to advance and promote themselves at the expense of others placed upon them by those cultural contracts that are based upon the honour and integrity of those that enter into them, then this individual self transcends those physical and intellectual limitations that naturally arise from that self being in itself a detached and differentiated entity, and that self becomes an absolute reality that is not only a valuable and irreplaceable part of their family and of their nation, but of creation and life itself, for only then can the self be truly considered to be fully alive.

Those that transcend their own physical and mental limitations by coalescing with other living creatures to create united cultural concepts of how to honour and respect that which sets us apart from all other living organisms are then able to freely function as they were designed to.

This free functioning of individuals then permits them to decide how best to share out the commonwealth to be found upon this planet and it permits them the freedom to decide between the self or others or to strike a fair balance between individual needs and the needs of others.

This freedom of choice can only become an absolute freedom if the decisions that the individual self makes are independent to and uninfluenced by any political, religious, economic or military pressures.

If the individual self is thus truly free to decide, then this entity has the chance to become immortal because unselfish acts in themselves are never forgotten and those that make them will always be remembered and recognised and thought of as they were when they made that decision to forgo themselves for the sake of their culture.

Accordingly, when decisions are made and those decisions and promises so to act are honoured, then a true situation arises and thus an absolute truth is created. These absolute truths therefore depend entirely upon the honour of the individual that creates the conditions necessary for such truths to exist and thus when it is stated that a gentleman's word is 'his bond' then this is an essential truth and forms the bedrock upon which all great cultures arise.

It is therefore only true men, those gentle and honourable creatures that nature has designed and created, that alone can create truly worthwhile and justifiable cultures that alone can possess the intellectual integrity to create codes of conduct that ensure that all living creatures are treated with that affection and respect that all life deserves.

The true culture of an individual is the culture of all individuals, no differentiation being possible between one individual and all individuals. No mathematical interpretation of validity is possible. Accordingly, any system of governing living creatures that depends upon mathematical probabilities or relationships is seriously flawed if that system is used to decide how such living organisms are to lead their lives.

If therefore a culture is and can be represented by and through anyone or all or some of its members then being above a mathematical or numerical interpretation of validity then the truths that such a culture deals in and with are those timeless, everlasting truths and thus it is the duty of all cultures to encapsulate those timeless and eternal truths into useable and accessible forms that can be accessed every second and every minute of every day that this planet continues to exist.

These timeless and inalienable truths are your cultural heritage and exist so that mankind can transform them into usable and accessible forms in order that humans may construct universally benevolent cultures which cherish and protect all forms of life for it is upon the respect for all forms of life that the salvation of the moral and intellectual integrity of mankind depend.

To believe that the power that created the intellectual capacity within man created it for no particular reason is to remain wilfully ignorant of its power and capacity to create and construct useful and beneficial systems of educating and protecting those fragile structures upon which all humans depend for their civilisation and which all other living creatures depend for their ultimate survival.

No creator or universally benevolent culture worth their salt would willingly tolerate the injustices and bigoted violence that plagues this planet. Just as religions give god a bad name, then so do corrupt and deformed party propagandists give politics a bad reputation for being totally incapable of curing the stupidity and greed that lie at the very heart of that mindless tribalistic aggression that haunts every moment of our waking lives.

God, unable to act to help or save us, depends entirely upon what we as his chosen intellectual representatives decide upon. To believe otherwise would be to believe that some creative power would be so incompetent and inept as to design a universe with a planet with greedy, ignorant, antagonistic war mongering disease ridden apes cluttering its surface whose only pleasure in life appeared to be to destroy, pollute, murder and control other living creatures whilst rampaging around attempting to satisfy their uncontrollable desires and lust for power, prestige and glory, such a belief is beyond belief itself.

To be then told that this is everybody's fault because of some original sin that someone somewhere for some reason committed, the exact nature of which cannot be revealed and further that if you do not believe this that you will be condemned to rot and suffer in some perpetual torment is a form of religious terrorism that keeps many people in a state of fear and uncertainty which coupled to that fear and uncertainty created by the politically endorsed economic and social terror tactics employed by decadent democracies to keep their slaves slaving to provide sustenance for the parasitic elite, then this combination has, throughout time, been proven sufficient in itself to keep people from demanding and getting their absolute right to live as truly free living organisms with an absolute right to food, shelter and warmth and an absolute right to have a choice between political, religious, economic, social and environmental systems or to choose to live without any preconceived, pre-arranged, predestined or pre-established peculiarly non-representative systems of ordering people about.

However, to be of any use at all individuals require a format by and through which they can express themselves. An individual's culture is that format by and through which he is granted those necessary freedoms to fully express the very essence of his being. It provides not only the tools but the knowledge on how to use those tools in order that that individual can skilfully reproduce his ideas and emotions into useable and accessible forms.

These forms coalesce and fuse with other useable, useful and accessible forms to create an understanding of how best mankind can protect and safeguard its most precious gifts; an awareness of ourselves and an awareness of time; this understanding being further refined into and expressed by and through codes of conduct that are designed to civilise and coordinate the efforts of mankind so as to avoid it turning upon itself and its other passengers upon this planet and ripping them and itself apart in a wild frenzy of tribalistic protectionism fuelled by incompetence, stupidity and greed.

It cannot be any other entity's fault if we use and abuse what we have been freely given. Our true creator has already given us all that we need, for he has given us the ability to discern those truths and realities that are necessary for mankind to function correctly and he has given true men the intellectual ability to convert those necessary truths into useful and viable forms.

Clearly it is the duty of all men to become true men, this transition from mindless drones to free and creative entities permitting them to convert their newly discovered reality into a culture that creates a just and fair society for all and every living creature in order that they may lead meaningful, productive and thus enjoyable lives.

The moral and spiritual health and thus the honour of a nation rests entirely upon its willingness to allow true men the opportunity to create universally benevolent cultures.

The rocks and stones that lie beneath your feet have existed for countless eons and will continue for countless ages when you leave, for they are locked in a time and space that controls nothing and that possesses no relative or absolute values whatsoever.

But it is that individual supported by and held up by those stones and rocks, that transient and delicate fleeting structure that through their culture decide the future, decide what heaven and hell will be, for such ideas, as now understood and represented, can never exist as true realities because neither heaven nor hell can possess any real or absolute truths in themselves, for their reality is yet to be decided. Their reality has not yet been decided because you the individual who must to understand what is being said, you yourself must exist as a time related entity that is aware of yourself, aware of others, aware of yourself relative to others and aware of yourself relative to the stones and rocks that support you and the lumps of wood and glass that surround you.

This awareness to decide is fundamental to existence for it allows and permits the self the choice to decide that reality by which it needs to live and exist.

Heaven or hell cannot as yet exist for whatever happens in either place would be relative to whatever created or controlled them.

But as you do not presently exist in either, other than that living hell that is only possible if you live in an environment almost entirely controlled by others, then heaven or hell can only be relative truths because the whole absolute relativity of either is irreversibly changed when another entity arrives to cast their vote either for or against.

When the self dies, it loses its absolute control over itself and becomes a fixed entity just like the rocks and stones. Having lost its most precious gifts of awareness of self and time it must agree with whatever is said or done for it no longer has any choice no matter how absurd or ridiculous then what you are told must be agreed with because thought is no longer possible because you have no time left to think.

The whole point of the intellect is to let you think those thoughts that the existence of time makes possible in order that you yourself can become, in yourself, a unique and irreplaceable easily recognised spiritual entity that cannot be denied by any devil or god for both have been denied themselves that opportunity that time gives us to become other than what we are told we are by others.

When the individual is given those essential spiritual and physical freedoms that only true cultures can supply, those essential freedoms permit the individual to construct a set of rational and educated set of ideals which after some thought and consideration will be used to form that choice that will be used to cast their vote when confronted either by oblivion or their true creator.

Our true creator is not the judge and jury! We are! And our true creator cannot avenge the stupidity and incompetence of mankind for vengeance is ours alone and depends upon those well thought out choices that only time makes possible.

Thus true vengeance is that retribution exacted by those living creatures that when confronted by their tormentors and jailers in a spiritual world of equality, justice and fairness in which our creator acts as an impartial referee then when those that live at the expense of others are asked to account for their actions, we as individual entities, educated and nurtured by those truths and realities that are as much a part of us as our brains and our bones, and are our cultural heritage, then it is we who decide the fate of others.

Once we cast our votes then this retribution, this taking back unto ourselves of that which has been taken illegally, this act will condemn those that perpetrated such acts to literally cease to exist as spiritual entities and thus their worst nightmare will become a reality.

Denied any form of recognition those that we condemn will return to that nothingness that awaits all those that do not truly exist in the first place for such entities are only relative to and only defined by their greed, their possessions and their inability to leave other living creatures alone.

It is your culture and your culture alone that gives you the time, the opportunity, the space, the resources, the tools, the knowledge, the experience, the love, the affection, the moral and the intellectual authority to become other than what you are and thus define what you will become.

There is a story often told which has already been given but it is given again to enforce its meaning.

The self is two young children, a little boy and girl, playing at the water's edge and seeing the river raging and swollen by storms delight in casting stones and sticks into its frothing turbulence. The boy's little sister slips and is swept away and the little lad fearing nothing leaps to save her.

It is not the inevitable consequences that matter, it is not the fault of anyone, it is irrelevant where this happened, it does not matter in which year or at what time of day, it cannot be important what others now say or do, it is the very act of leaping forward that is the absolute reality that promises those that make it immortal.

The act cannot be denied for it is an absolute fact. Cultures exist and must exist in order that those sacrificial acts that the self makes in order to become immortal are not squandered or wasted or end in futile recriminatory squabbles that descend into hatred, fear and violence.

Cultures exist so that whatever sacrifices the self makes become part of life, become part of death and ultimately decide the fate of both.

Cultures must exist to avoid people wasting their most precious and irreplaceable gifts in that daily drudgery of slaving to keep the parasitic elite cosy in their exclusive developments to greed and incompetence whilst attempting to keep their heads above water surrounded by noise, pollution and cultural deprivation.

Any creator no matter how vindictive or power mad must be bound by his creations for that is the purpose for and the reason why the intellect was created in the first instance.

As such then the creative power of the intellect as exemplified by the culture that it creates is directly responsible for deciding what a creator's creations will become.

21 Fearing Nothing – Fearing All

THE SMALL CHILD fearing nothing can be you.

But the small child fails to save his sister because he is too young, he cannot be aware yet despite all of this he has become a true reality, he has acted despite the cost, despite the consequences.

No matter how foolish the act he is envied because to live without one's friend, to live without that which makes life worth living, is not to live or be alive at all. To live without a culture, to live without the means to be free, to live a remote and isolated existence, denied that friendship and affection that alone can be given to you by and through your culture is not to be alive at all but to be an individual that simply exists clinging to what little they have, fearing all and thus easy prey to those parasitic maggots that infest humanity with their greed and usury, their political and moral incompetence, their religious dogmatism and their one world theories that deny others those rights and freedoms necessary for the self to become immortal.

If mankind uses its allotted time upon this planet to create cultures founded upon justice, fairness, equality and honour then this is what will await mankind both upon this planet and elsewhere.

If one uses and if one is permitted to use one's time wisely then the transition from a materiel form to a non-material form will barely be noticed because in the very essence of creative acts, and encapsulated in those pleasures feelings and thoughts, is a feeling of total freedom and beingness that transcends time, place and space and though the possibility so to act may never arise again one comes as close to a feeling of immortality that it is possible to experience upon this planet.

Death in itself therefore can be treated as a creative act neither fearing all nor fearing nothing.

Great cultures fearing nothing themselves teach that death can be and should be a creative act that one must be fully prepared for in order that this recreation of the self into a non-time related form should be a smooth transition from one understood reality to another.

The cultures that we create upon this planet can not only bind people together but can bind our creator to honour those cultural codes and

cultural contracts that its members have decided are just and fair representations of reality and thus are proper and legitimate intellectual constructs
by which and through which it is possible to organise people into a system
of civilised and sociable living.

Clearly if mankind were permitted to function as common sense and our
rationality tell us is correct then this planet would have no need for those
particular and peculiarly non-essential political and religious systems that
have mysteriously arisen to control them.

Once trapped and enslaved by the constant need to struggle to survive
then decadent political and religious systems can hold the essentials of life
up for ransom and being painfully aware that if true men were left to their
own devices they would recreate great and coherent cultures that would
render their own pathetic and transient non-essential intellectual constructs
obsolete, decadent political and religious systems obtain a perverse pleasure
in destroying and polluting all and every culturally legitimate means to challenge their perpetual grasp upon power and control.

The voids created within nations that have had their cultural heritage
destroyed and polluted by lies and misrepresentations of reality need to be
filled with any old trash, yet deep within the lives of those lost souls that
wander those dark and lonely alleyways created by greed and stupidity,
there lies a deep, almost limitless, emptiness that no amount of westernised
cartoon culture or chemically enriched consumerism can fill.

To distract the distressed, decadent democracies and their chronically
outdated religions, devise a daily diet of trouble and strife, division and hardship, degradation and disease, these being essential tools in their armoury to
dismantle the culture of those nations they control and yet when they finally
succeed and are able to sit back in their bomb proof bunkers and preside
over that sickening dance to the death that all societies go through when
they have had their cultural safeguards forcibly removed they begin to fear
that others have come to see them for what they are and thus they scour
the globe for any other culture that despises those western ideals that have
become as pathetic and ridiculous as their cartoon replacement cultures.

Once the intellectual capacity of man has been destroyed by making him
grovel for his existence, he reverts to one of those wild irrational animals
that needs to be chained and enslaved thus justifying the pretentious needs
of others to control them.

But when a culture dies and humans tear each other apart using that religious, political and gender ridden tribalism that arises when fear conspires with that jealousy of others that greed and stupidity fosters and creates, then to hide those vile and tattered remnants of those selves that were once honourable, just and fair, decadent nations and their self-appointed elitist regimes murder and mutilate others to try to hide their own ignominy and shame from themselves.

The world thus becomes dominated by political and religious systems that must employ 'relative to themselves and nobody else' relative truths and when the validity of those truths is challenged or questioned then such systems either revert to mindless indiscriminate violence or that slimy secrecy upheld as relevant by numerical and statistical misinformation, and failing all else an appeal to some god given right to be right even when plainly and obviously wrong.

Such systems having founded their religious and political philosophies entirely upon the elitist 'us and them' principles come to believe that they have a divine right to abuse others. They force themselves to believe that this is how it was meant to be because they possess no cultural criteria of correctness that would immediately demonstrate to them that their religious and political philosophies are as absurd as they are.

However they are keenly aware that they are acting beyond their abilities and not being able to truly justify their absurd lack of moral and intellectual authority to act the way that they do they resort to brute force and a culturally irrelevant smoke screen of two dimensional cardboard cartoon cut-outs having a wonderful and jolly time reinforced by electronically controlled forced laughter, the volume and intensity of which is designed to tell the natives not only what is funny but to educate them as to how amusing it was, yet the only funny thing about the whole sad affair is that it is not funny at all.

One can laugh and be amused yet a bitter after taste and an emptiness persist so much so that many are forced to eat and eat in a futile attempt to fill those cultural voids that such false fun and happiness leave behind after the forced laughter fades away.

When a nation resorts to brute force to get its own way and when it resorts to importing its culture and when it resorts to overfeeding its prisoners and slaves with junk and trash and when it refuses to give a free choice as to what political system, if any, its citizens want to be made relative to, then a form of democratised terrorism results in which, like their fetish for figures and having lived their lives in a cartoon culture, anything is possible, and being numerically possible and morally and ethically validated by one monkey having more paper promises than another then whatever it is must, not only be justified, but must be true.

Accordingly true men who possess the intellectual ability to ridicule such beliefs must be rendered ineffectual and powerless by the use of illegitimate and repressive laws that make all acts of dissention a crime.

Naturally democratised terrorists hide not only behind slimy secrecy but claim that these culturally, morally and ethically illegitimate reforms that they push through are to protect us from those that they are busy murdering and mutilating so that they can destroy their cultures and replace them with diseased democracies that will espouse the same non-essential tripe about how well we are all doing even though it is clear that whilst western democracies have become numerically rich the quality of life has become so poor that great swaths of their populations have become obese and depressed by that inner emptiness that haunts all those who only live to eat, work and breath.

The populations of such nations are bombarded with noisy information and colourful distractions to stop them thinking too deeply and even if they did, being powerless landless peasants with no absolute rights, they would be unable to act upon their own conclusions.

Becoming mentally sick and physically dependent upon their gaolers they turn upon themselves and others in a futile attempt to improve the quality of their lives.

As a result, love, honour, respect and tolerance are replaced by a jealous hatred and fear of others who appear uncontaminated by greed and pride of possessions and appear to live quite happily muddling along.

But muddling along cannot be quantified, photographed, DNA'd, measured or controlled; it cannot be made subservient to the political and economic needs of those mentally unstable deranged democracies that have convinced themselves that others must be told about and forced to agree with.

As a result, the leaders of decadent democracies announce that it is imperative for the safety of their world that they trample upon and ignore all forms of civilised behaviour in their frenzied attempts to bring other cultures into alignment with their myopic and distorted imagery of what their theoretical one world super democracy should look like.

Accordingly, love is replaced by jealousy, respect is replaced by indifference, tolerance is replaced by violence and honour is replaced by a chauvinistic military pride in past and present exploits which justifies the elite and their hired henchmen to squander yet more of the planet's resources and commonwealth upon yet more culturally meaningless and ineffectual military hardware.

One cannot exhort such war mongering nations to 'love thy neighbour' because to them love means 'that which pleases' and as it obviously pleases them to go around bashing people up and terrorising them with obscenely discriminatory laws and indiscriminately destructive weaponry then that is what they will continue to do.

22 Love Thy ... ?

LOVE, TRUE LOVE, is that disinterested affection that living creatures display and feel towards one another. Its opposite is antagonism – the interference with and in the growth and well-being of another living organism.

True love, as expressed in cultural terms, is not only a display and feeling of disinterested affection, but has at its very core the idea of 'reciprocity', that is, this feeling is worthy of respect and thus is worthy of some form of acknowledgement through and by a similar feeling being reciprocated by utilising established cultural practices.

The duty that befalls all cultures that possess a truly disinterested affection for their members is to open up and form channels of communication by and through which all living creatures can not only communicate with each other but by and through which they can coalesce and form united and idealised representations of that reality and purpose in life that they have in common.

The degree to which people are empowered and assisted to freely communicate and discuss issues and ultimately to form freely available alternatives to those that cannot, or will not, or choose not, to join in with that culture that they disagree with is that by which the cultural credibility of a nation can be measured.

A nation that wishes to be culturally creditworthy therefore needs to have strict codes of conduct to ensure that its credibility is not compromised by those who possess no honour or shame and that would use and abuse such channels of communication for their own improper and seedy purposes.

All cultures founded upon justice and fairness would as a matter of principle issue each of its members with a cultural credit card that not only gives them a unique cultural copyright but identifies their cultural creditworthiness.

The card would be a record of the degree of understanding of the intellectual, moral and ethical responsibilities that the owner needed to uphold in order that their culture could function smoothly and correctly and without the need for constant and excessive enforcement of its codes of conduct.

Those codes of conduct would be the first concepts that a person would be required to learn, understand and put into practice and would take precedence over all other disciplines.

Members of a culture would be educated to appreciate the value of possessing a high degree of cultural credibility because it is upon this that their honour and the honour of their nation depends.

Once an individual achieves an honourable status then they in themselves represent those cultural laws necessary to ensure justice and fairness and such is the honour that can be conferred upon their cultural credibility that they can achieve those cultural privileges that make them truly free – freedom from arrest upon trivial and untested, or unfounded allegations, freedom of speech, freedom of thought, freedom of movement and the freedom to know the cultural credibility of all those individuals, organisations, producers and political movements that do or could affect the quality of their life or their environment.

Just as there are several types of truth there are also several types of information and in decadent societies most of the information that is made available is of little or no use. However, to pretend that it is such societies develop an obsession with indoctrinating people from the year dot with useless information in order that they can become highly informed yet culturally isolated and lonely state owned and controlled individuals that have had their cultural identity stolen from them and their cultural copyright filed away in order to blackmail them in later life to pay back to the state what the state has taken from them without their permission. Thus, as then, as now – a handful of beads and some worthless paper promises for the heart and soul of a living creature. The culture of a nation is there to educate individuals on how 'to think' and not 'what to think'.

In decadent cultures apart from having to get into debt to the state, either literally or by implication, even those who are educated at university level display a limited capacity to reason correctly or effectively because they are forced to use their time in accruing unto themselves enough information to satisfy others that they know everything and yet understand nothing. Naturally this makes them ideal candidates to go out and rip people off and pay themselves daft money for being more inefficient and more incompetent than the competition.

But in nations with sick and weedy cultures that employ ill-educated well-informed debt-ridden rip off merchants to run their decadent democracies there is no such thing as real competition because that which everyone strives for, and those objects that are touted as being desirable and life enhancing are yours already and if you are stupid enough to pay for them again then so be it. However, the idea that life is some form of competition, a struggle to survive and it is the financially fittest who will win, this daft concept must be driven in to the minds of people in order that they at least get out of bed. But what do the winners win? Intelligence? Love? Wisdom? Immortality?

It is up to the culture of a nation to educate its offspring to be honourable, affectionate, universally loving and tolerant individuals who possess that understanding and wisdom that demonstrates that to win the honour and respect of other living creatures and thus to gain and keep cultural credibility is the greatest prize of all.

In humans unmodified by creative, strong, just and fair cultural codes of conduct their animal instincts restrict love and affection to their own group or tribe, thus in tribal lands gross acts of barbarism can be enacted at the will of a few who believe that this restriction of love and affection and goodwill was ordained by some mythical being who came to them in a dream dressed as a crocodile and if such beliefs are allowed to persist and acts of tribal barbarism are left unchallenged then such beliefs can incite tribal instincts and fears which often escalate into a wild frenzy of self-interested protectionism known as genocide.

It is only the culture of a nation that can protect people from modern day tribalism. In nations that possess strong cultures and strong codes of conducting their affairs the parasitic usurer and profiteer, the polluter and the political deviants would be held in check by a public outrage and ridicule that such self-centred ignominious scum have had the audacity to try and usurp that authority that belongs to every single living creature to possess their fair share of this planet and then to have the cheek to try to dish it back out in paltry dollops whilst they themselves join their mates in their tribal strongholds to pay each their obscenely disproportionate awards for being such culturally irrelevant filth, this sort of vile behaviour would put such people in a cultural classification below that of disease ridden microbes.

But in nations that possess no culture or have replaced what little they had with a cartoon culture in which anything is possible then such cultural deviants can become iconic figures that can blatantly celebrate their financial superiority, no matter how achieved, by using their paper promises to dispossess others by buying up disproportionate amounts of objects that turn them into those celebrities that become the envy of those that are unknowingly and unwittingly paying the price for elevating some at the expense of others.

Thus the whole culture of a nation can begin to revolve around those trivial and tawdry dramas as to who has got what and in which people are judged by which ghetto to greed they inhabit and how much time they spend trying to regain some honour and dignity by adopting 'good causes' whilst trying desperately to become 'normal' by appearing in those pointless and meaningless embarrassments that are to fill the void between one sickeningly empty moment and the next, this new culturally divisive medium being known as television.

In cultures founded upon numerical wealth any cardboard cut-out of reality that appeared on television to tell the culturally oppressed how wonderful it is to be superior must be superior, must be happy, must be clever because the numbers cannot lie, they cannot be wrong, and they must add up to a world which all must aspire to reach.

In cultures founded upon the need to display a disinterested affection to all living creatures and not just to particular groups or tribes or particular individuals numerical wealth counts for nothing because numerical wealth tends to completely destroy the quality of life to be found in a nation because numerical wealth allows and permits an individual's interpretation of 'how things should be' to become 'how things are' irrespective of the damage caused to others and their environment.

If individuals are encouraged by their culture to display a disinterested affection to all other living creatures and to respect their environment, then this limitation of a natural desire to possess more than it is right or healthy to have will free that individual to pursue a proper and worthwhile existence.

Disinterested means unselfish, generous and impartial and thus not favouring one more than another. Affectionate means kindly disposed towards and acting in a non-discriminatory manner and if this unselfish, generous and impartial kindness is extended to all creation then we possess true love.

If our creator is not only the totality of all truths but also possesses a true love for his creations then he cannot favour one individual, tribe or nation more than another. To pretend that it could be otherwise is to be wilfully ignorant of the purpose and meaning of life and existence itself.

It is necessary for any creator, if they are to be more than just wishful thinking and to be based solely upon a blind acceptance of obscure and improbable claims, to furnish the intellect of his creations with a constancy and a power that enables it to construct meaningful ideas and concepts and to allow it sufficient time to reach rational well-balanced conclusions.

Thus, our creator, be it nature or whatever, must have within itself those absolute truths to which we as parts of creation must possess in ourselves to varying degrees. If our creator is the totality of Truth, Love and Constancy then they must also possess Wisdom, that is, the ability to understand how existence has to be arranged in order for it to function as intended and to make that understanding available to those creatures that exist within and are the purpose for that creation.

Those creatures within creation that are aware of themselves are also directly aware of those responsibilities and duties that arise from possessing the ability to be truthful and loving entities that use time wisely and that educate and refine their intellects in order that they become those creative and competent entities upon which the future of mankind depend.

Humans therefore require an environment in which the truth is always available to them and in which they have the protection and affection of their fellow men and in which they are given that time and that place that belongs to them and no others. Within this cultural sanctuary they are given a constant reality that cannot and does not change, for this reality must be non-relative to whichever bunch of subnormals are bullying and controlling the rest of mankind.

From this cultural sanctuary individuals are able to come to terms with themselves and thus can begin to comprehend the meanings and uses of wisdom, truth and love and can then progress to join in to create stable and constant intellectually active environments that make true thoughts possible.

It is the culture of a nation that is responsible for creating those physical and spiritual environments that all humans require if they are to become anything more than factory fodder or money grabbers.

It is only the culture of a nation that alone can possess the intellectual authority to make universally legitimate pronouncements concerning social, political and religious issues because it is only the culture of a nation, if it has one, that is the sum total of man's objective analysis of reality and its formation into verifiable, usable and accessible forms that can be used to justify their actions.

These usable and accessible forms possess an apodictic certainty that puts them above contradiction and thus they become those axioms that define reality and thus these axiomatic certainties become that criteria through and by which all realities are judged.

This cultural criteria of correctness defines the common sense of a nation because common sense depends upon the common notions of a nation and the common notions, or beliefs of a nation, are totally dependent upon its culture which is directly dependent upon the intellectual skill and honour of its artisans. If therefore a nation has no true men with the intellectual skill and honour to create just, fair and equitable social structures then it will possess no true culture and thus having no criteria to judge its own actions will degenerate into an inconstant and transient politically dominated state in which no true freedoms are possible.

Worse still there will be no cultural constraints or safeguards to keep the sectarian bigot and the political and financial parasites in check so that the peoples of such nations become lonely universally isolated individuals completely at the mercy of the state which then proceeds to control every aspect of their lives.

Having no culture of their own makes such nations unable to grasp the wider implications of their own illegitimate acts of aggression against others because they do not have any universally acceptable channels of communication and thus resort to brute force and threats.

The peoples of such nations thus turn in towards themselves and their supposed allies. Being universally reviled for their obscene and culturally illegitimate acts of self-interested aggression they are forced to trade in and swap their sick and deranged ideas and cultures with each other, so much so, that this intellectual incestuous relationship leads to such a blinkered outlook that such nations come to believe their own inadequate conclusions based upon half understood and misrepresented versions of those political and religious realities that aren't particularly real in the first instance.

Thus, they come to believe that there is only one world because, like a cart horse blinkered so as not to be distracted, they adopt a type of tunnel vision and then no amount of rational discussion or persuasion can change their minds.

The populations of nations that are led by leaders who are blinded by their own political propaganda and whose minds are set solidly for a particular vision in which this planet has to be shoehorned into their version of reality are subjected to so much state interference that they quickly become morose and apathetic to such a degree that all they can talk about is money, that and how much their cultural hovels are worth, how much things cost and how much they made that week or if this drivel dries up, what they had for dinner or what they are going to watch on their televisions.

When the population becomes sufficiently intellectually dysfunctional the parasitic elite and the military supremists can then, by goading them or others to lash out occasionally, can then indulge in extreme acts of economic and social tribalism in which they enrich and entrench themselves further into the fabric of a nation by pretending that they are absolutely necessary to safeguard their citizens from that terrorism that they daily practise upon others.

Being bullies and thus cowards they squeal with a self-righteous hypo-critical indignation if those that they daily dispossess, and bully so much as defend themselves or their cultures from those illegal and illegitimate acts that have become the hallmark of those western degenerates who force their demented democratic dictatorships upon others.

These numerically based dictatorships have become nothing more than a seedy and pathetic misrepresentation of reality using the illogical self-rela-tive truths of numerical relationships that theoretically require vast numbers to justify their use yet unilateral declarations of intent are often based upon a few semi-literate miseducated and misinformed zombified state owned and controlled serfs who show their gratitude by voting their jailers back into power and thus give them an unlimited mandate to continue to pollute and terrorise this planet.

Thus, nations can easily become infested with control freaks and money junkies who develop a fetish for possessions that then require extensive private properties thus spawning an entire race of people who become addicted to getting into debt to afford their tin and plasterboard prisons which contain those objects which represent the totality of their culturally worthless and miserable lives and which must be guarded at all costs. Thus the money lender, the usurer, and the insurers rub their hands with glee for they realise that once this type of self-interested, self-preservation, tribalistic instinct kicks in then that fear of loss devalues and demeans people until they become less than human and this sense of fear cannot be eradicated because they no longer possess the cultural means to re-establish control over their own lives.

Accordingly, as their world fragments around them they become those lonely culturally isolated individuals whose lives have become a pointless and meaningless struggle to survive.

23 Revelations

THE SOUL OF man, trapped in the body of an ape, is that force which transmits what the senses sense and transfers that information to the intellect where in a space created by awareness of itself it is analysed by logical and rational processes which form those inputs into understandable ideas and concepts.

The intellect therefore is totally dependent upon how things are presented to it – it cannot prearrange what has been chosen by others for it to be shown until it reaches that stage of development whereby it can begin to judge for itself what it wants to think about. However, if what it would like to think about no longer exists or has not yet been created then it will be stuck with other people's choices, other people's beliefs and other people's accounts of reality. Such prearranged and established beliefs, choices and accounts are however rarely true because those accounts of reality that we receive from others are based upon belief systems that themselves are entirely dependent upon the cultural, spiritual and political control systems that others have pre-established in order to indoctrinate the young and gullible into accepting 'what is' and not necessarily 'what should be'.

Universally coherent, constant, creative and intellectually competent cultures however are not subjective systems of educating or advising the young or gullible, that is, they recognise that there is a proper time and a proper place for all things but it is not up to that culture to decide for that individual when any particular point in time or place is, can be or has to be achieved.

Being objective, universally acceptable and applicable intellectually competent entities they regard children as precious gifts that need to be carefully nurtured and thus they permit them to grow and develop and mature at their own pace for creative cultures realise that nature itself does not demand anything of us, it simply gives what it can and only asks that in return we do not indulge in that jealous greed that spoils things for others. It lets matters take their own course and it permits the innocent to discover and learn at their own pace, and it allows those freedoms necessary for people to decide which reality is true and which lifestyle is best for themselves; in other words, it has no preconceived plans regarding mankind – it simply provides a constancy of purpose and leaves people to their own devices.

However, to a particularly nasty and vicious breed of human inadequate leaving others to their own devices would seriously threaten to unhinge their already tenuous grasp upon reality and thus they thrash around wildly attempting to control their own emotional and intellectual instability. Such delinquents are finally forced to accrue to themselves like-minded culturally incompetent desperados who being similarly smitten by a jealous hatred of others who seem to be getting along alright without them embark upon mindless campaigns of vindictive retribution against anything that reminds them of their own inability to come to terms with that deep sense of spiritual and moral isolation that daily reminds them that they are nobodies going nowhere, because even their creator wouldn't be able to stand that foul stench that always accompanies those self-interested incompetents and those mindless busybodies as they attempt to reorder existence to suit their own inadequate conclusions regarding justice and fairness.

In their pathetic attempt to give some credence to their belief systems they are forced to invent new religions which obviously must be true because nobody can prove otherwise mainly because religion means to bind and as you end up being tied up and burnt or beheaded if you disagree it's probably best to keep quiet. Having established the one and only true religion in which every living person's cultural copyright now belonged to some manmade deity allowed the representatives upon earth to get their hands upon just about anything they wanted simply by 'claiming by naming'.

If others ignored their demented drivelling, then they simply plundered and pillaged those cultures that hadn't realised that the wealth they had was meant not to be shared out equally but actually belonged to some super being who had appointed a particularly well-armed guerrilla to look after it for them.

Because this system seemed to work so well the elite that arose by dispossessing others of their fair share began to believe in their own synthesised versions of reality. Unable to distinguish between analytic truths and synthetic truths led them to adopt a system of logic that didn't even bother attempting to establish whether anything was true or false, it simply had to decide whether or not a particular consequence could be justifiably deduced from a given set of inferences.

A sort of consequentialist type of thinking arose, the 'what if' line of reasoning that led to a whole new type of logic that was entirely based upon suppositional conditionals. This 'if I did this, then this might happen' world was to form the basis of the new sciences 'if I mix this with that then...' It was of no consequence to the new consequentialist cultures, or the new sciences that were arising, what the consequences to nature or the environment or to other people their actions were to have because they had already synthesised a new reality that had created a creator that had made them masters of the universe for no other particular reason than it was possible.

This absurdity became so established by brute force, fear and ignorance that no other intellectual forms of permitting people to come to terms with their own realities, that is, those actualities that were real to them but of no consequence to their ringmasters, were permitted to exist. Given no choice but to accept somebody else's reality they were often forced to deform their own natural instincts of justice, equality and fairness, this brutalisation of their consciences leading to a subhuman form of individual that having been broken and battered by the greed, stupidity and cultural elitism and incompetence of others would then have a gun shoved in their hand and then ordered to slaughter anything that did not conform to that synthesised reality stitched together out of the half understood and misrepresented cultural cast offs of other distant disreputable cultures that had shrivelled up and died because the finances to keep their henchmen paid eventually dried up.

To keep this synthesised reality in the realms of enforceable fantasy protected by a cocoon of inadequate and illogical state sponsored illegitimate reforms, the citizens were debarred from making any political or religious adjustments to their cultural environments unless they owned large tracts of mud and earth upon which they could construct exclusive and prodigious dwelling places to house those cultural artefacts that only the elite could afford.

Pressurised into acknowledging that other living creatures actually had a limited right to have a limited amount to say and that this limited amount of choice should be strictly limited to what the elite had previously chosen to be a correct and suitable limited number of choices and that these choices should be limited to a limited period of time and limited to some limited place such as a portacabin or church hall and that the choices would be limited to one thumb print or other symbolic scrawl and that this smudge or mark, to be valid, had to be singular and exactly within the limitations of one box only, this limitation of man's right to control his own environment, only being forced upon the elite after an unlimited number of men had been needlessly slaughtered in a vain and futile and prematurely incompetent attempt to create a one world super state that could and would dominate and control its members by that fear of force that is necessary to uphold all supremist regimes that depend upon a belief that some senile creator in the advanced stages of dementia had chosen a bunch of intellectual and moral delinquents to represent the totality of his creative abilities by putting them in control of creating a just fair all-inclusive stable and constant and loving environment for all his other creations upon a lump of rock on the edge of existence.

The cultures that such supremists were required to create were then of necessity ones that had to limit the choices of lifestyle and quality of life of those that weren't considered fit or suitable to join the elite and most importantly the elite must limit cultural education to their own sect in order to avoid the lower orders from acquiring those intellectual tools and blueprints that would enable them to not only think for themselves, and have something worthwhile to think about, but would cause them to demand the means and the power and the resources to make their conclusions a reality.

Accordingly a cardboard cut-out culture was created in which the supremacy of the elite was established by the extensive use of symbolic representations of the dominion that control junkies had over other living creatures, these iconic representations of their synthesised reality being heavily dependent upon crowns and lions, shields and swords, as well as a few mythical beasts but all requiring a figurehead, a one and only that must be obeyed, right or wrong, just or unjust, fair or unfair, clever or stupid, alive or dead, no choices in between, black or white, democracy or nothing, submit or starve, fight or die, no middle ground allowed, rich or poor, legal or illegal, heaven or hell, happy or sad, this two dimensional approach to reality, based upon the ancient ramblings of a bunch of half-wits who totally believed in everything either being one thing or the other with nothing in between, this belief system leading to a fixation with controlling and refining those objects at either end of a spectrum whilst ignoring and denying the reality of anything in between. Their whole world became a two dimensional one, an 'us' and 'them' society that required their inadequate conclusions based upon improper inferences to somehow be regarded as justifiable and verifiable substantive claims and thus their capitals became overrun with statues and temples in a bizarre attempt to legitimise the illegitimate denial of another world, a world of honour, justice and equality that could create a culture that could refine and civilise those basic animal instincts and control that stupid greed for distinction and success that condemned others to be enslaved.

To ensure another world could not arise they set about controlling this planet with lumps of paper and metal which had to be embossed and impressed with those two-dimensional cartoon images of the latest figurehead to be dangled in front of the rabble by the parasitic elite.

These figureheads, to make any sense at all, had to be somehow 'chosen' and to simplify this process all the minor deities were abandoned in favour of one almighty super being who then ordained the need for a spartanistic intellectual revolution the very essence of which was to despise culture and to encourage people to undertake outlandish acts of self-immolation which usually involved hacking everyone to death, including themselves, with lumps of steel.

Those living in the west in culturally sterile hovels held together by mud and snots became overwhelmed with and in admiration of a culture that by brute force and ignorance could convert their original culture into one that made some able to live at the top of the dung heap, with no questions asked and that could force others to carry all their needs and wants up to them. Thus, the west eagerly adopted a replacement culture that could be used by the elitist thugs to subdue others and this coupled to an even more enthusiastic adaptation of a religion that had as its emblem a cross under which gross acts of barbarism could be enacted, this synthesis mysteriously gave the new steel wielding culturally dead militaristic power freaks a god given right to control this planet.

Having gained control of the earth itself by brute force and a wilful ignorance of those civilising forces that our true creator had made available to all, they then began to forcibly import bits and pieces of other people's culture to fill the voids in their ever-increasing mansion houses.

To induce their own serfs to get out of bed they began selling back the land by printing paper promises embossed with the figurehead of the local potentate. The gullibility of the greedy ensured that countless numbers flocked to those areas in which these promises were being printed hoping to find a few square inches of mud upon which to settle.

It was discovered that by destabilising life by putting everything into motion, that this process could be rapidly speeded up and thus abstract promises of a better life just around the corner, promises that could not and would not be kept, induced people to relinquish their rights and abandon what little control they had over the essentials of life and rush about looking to their leaders in the capitol to give them that capital that would transform them into men of substance.

Everything had to be put in a state of flux, great engines needed to be constructed to power the wheels of this great cultural revolution in which everyone busied themselves eagerly awaiting the fulfilment of those promises of health, wealth and happiness that could only be achieved by capitulation to the state and its symbols of power and glory.

For their paper promises to have meaning they must like a cartoon be made to move, the faster and more uncontrollably the better because when they flick past faster than the eye can follow or the brain can calculate then the mind gives up and the eye watches television instead.

Once the supersonic speed of state sponsored greed is reached such paper promises, overworked and overheated by countless money grabbers over inflating the value of such worthless abstractions, unable to go any faster eventually melt and transmutate into a form of plastic which can then be moulded into those symbols of financial liberation that are essential in keeping the slaves slaving in some culturally isolated backwater, drifting aimlessly around with no secure anchorage or safe harbour, slowly capsizing under the weight of their own cultural and spiritual insignificance and weighed down further by being in debt to those shady and abstract notions that completely control their lives.

Any living creature born into the chrome and plastic red tape of the financial and cultural unrealities of modernism is immediately in debt, the consequences of their entry into life already calculated, their identity already stolen, their cultural copyright already sold to the highest bidder, their council tax bill pre-prepared, their debt to society mounting daily, all in order that those plastic and paper cardboard cut-out symbols of somebody else's financial reality can be seen to move, can be seen to put the slaves into motion, can be seen to control life itself as long as the hidden costs to honour, justice, love, affection, tolerance and the quality of life are hidden behind those slimy secrets that belong to the political elite and their cronies in commerce.

When whole nations begin to drift aimlessly from one universal culturally irrelevant moment to the next then their cartoon cultures must be cranked up yet another gear so as to generate a false sense of going or getting somewhere. Having given up watching paper promises fly past at inordinate speed beyond their grasp and having accepted the inalienable right of the already rich to get richer by paying themselves and their cronies obscenely disproportionate wages, because it is possible to do so, because there aren't any cultural safeguards left, those watching their favourite cultural cabinet of colourful wonders are forced to either watch imported high speed renditions of unreality in which the camera jumps from one lump of rehearsed rubbish to another before the ridiculousness of the whole becomes apparent or they are presented with the opportunity to suffer a slow and insidious lobotomisation by following the drab and dreary antics of one ape desperately trying to impress another by a series of prearranged and pathetic attempts to be 'outrageous' and 'controversial' both at the same time.

Thus, anything becomes possible because the speed of delivery of the one and the slow drip and drop of the other leads to a false sense of constancy, the intellect and senses having been lulled to such a catatonic state that they will accept any new information with that blank indifference that their moral and intellectual stupor makes inevitable.

Accordingly interspersed with and in this cultural drivel are the brash and brazen sycophantic twitterings of your friendly neighbourhood rip-off merchants who are busy spending your hard earned paper promises trying to convince you that what appears before your traumatised and by this time uncoordinated higher mental abilities are actually worth possessing or the mind is presented with the latest series of atrocities carried out in your name using your share of this planet's common wealth, these insane attempts to control others being based upon consequences of a cartoon culture, which being a synthesis of unjustifiable unrealities in the first instance makes anything into a possible reality.

But to the insane everything is not only possible but to be expected and thus accepted with the same degree of uninterested disinterest. If it is numerically possible then it must also be electronically, scientifically and medically possible even if so improbable as not to be of any significance. But this is of no consequence to the consequentialist cultures because their truths are not absolute or logical or moral or ethical truths, they are those self-relative synthetic truths that are synthesised to justify the stupidity, greed, inefficiency and incompetence of the ruling elite and their culturally irrelevant and disposable political systems.

But when relative truths are given the force of absolute truths by the illegitimate and illegal use of force of arms and the use of intellectual terrorism that states all public thoughts are state owned and controlled thoughts and thus must be modified, changed or cease to exist then the relative truths of one nation can and do become historical truths. Historical truths must then become mathematical truths and to be mathematical truths require 'numbers' but to be really, really true they require 'a number'. Once the number has been decided upon it must be truer than true and thus to deny its validity becomes a criminal offence.

Being a criminal offence to deny this number makes the individual bound by a numerical interpretation of reality. Worse still if they deny the number and possessing no absolute freedoms and their cultural copyright being public property, the state can unleash the bloodhounds of their inquisition to wreak an uncontrollable vengeance upon those that deny the supremacy not only of the state to create this number but also the use that it puts such a number to.

From this line of reasoning the whole planet belongs to those that can claim it by naming it, measuring it, numbering it and classifying it and then moving on to it. The problem with numbers is you don't really have any true choice; in fact, you can only choose one number or another which is no choice at all. The problem with number based cultures and their consequentialist thinking patterns is that people live in fear of the consequences of their own actions yet when the inevitable happens as a direct consequence of those very actions their cartoon cultures cannot cope and therefore instead of attempting to cure or remove those that cause others to react badly to their lives being maliciously interfered with by a bunch of power mad elitist morons they revert to counting the dead, counting the cost in financial terms and counting the hours and minutes until they unleash yet again a mindlessly indiscriminate campaign of unjustified and misdirected retribution at those that refuse to bow down to illegitimate unilateral declarations of malignant intent to destroy others in an obscenely disproportionate manner because of course the 'us and them' elitist mind fix of the intellectually subnormal having no cultural criteria of correctness always count the 'us' as being infinitely more valuable and worthy than the 'them' who are obviously expendable or else their god would have made 'them' into 'us'.

Without greed there would be little to fear and therefore no need for numbers, but certain nations do not possess the intellectual skills to understand or to cope with the need to isolate the irrationality of living by the inevitable consequences of confusing emotionally based animal instincts with universally valid intellectually based conclusions. Accordingly vast armadas of highly trained and equipped henchmen must now include the obligatory female who because of the highly charged emotional conflicts of interest between the intellect and the animal instincts that will arise must be shoved to the front in the hope that they will be killed or captured and thus demonstrate how despicable and barbarous are the 'them' and thus the 'them' deserved to be murdered and mutilated in the first place. These armadas are sent out to ensure that all must bow down to the golden calf of capitalism and consumerism and must doff their hats to those degraded and degenerate democratic dictators who tout their antiquated and intellectually senile political systems as being the one and only method of universal recognition and thus salvation.

These less than human examples of that grotesque distortion of reality that happens when stupidity and greed are mixed with ignorance and fear and are then compounded with a quantitative analysis of who deserves what only survive because there are no cultural safeguards left because men are no longer truly free and without true freedom we cannot have true thoughts and without true thoughts we cannot have true intentions and without true intentions we cannot have any honour and without honour we cannot have justice and equality.

Without justice and equality, we cannot create a universal culture capable of reuniting mankind into one brotherhood of man possessing those ideals and principles that are the purpose for and the meaning of life itself.

24 Towards the Edge

IN MODERN, CULTURALLY sterile nations in which their parasitic politicians are up to their necks in debt to their cronies in commerce that use them to ensure that the entire population are up to their necks in debt then it is only a matter of time before an incestuous relationship develops between the state and its economic and political systems whereby the politicians force the state to not only fund their deranged fantasies but also to bear the full cost of convincing the general population that these flights of fancy will indeed improve the quality of their lives.

Accordingly, the public will not only be forced to pay for those surplus to requirements political embarrassments, either directly or indirectly, but will also be required to pay for their propaganda machines.

A type of politically deformed mutant will thus be spawned that cannot be eradicated, such self-seeking slugs clinging tenaciously to power whilst eating the heart out of all that that makes existence worthwhile and tolerable.

This mutation from what were originally intended to be self-supporting individuals displaying an independent and free thinking attitude towards the affairs of man and being honourably charged with acting for the common good, this transformation into state funded party propagandists controlled by bribery and corruption and by a pressing need to become slum landlords will make the transition from the direct inefficiency of your local non-representative representative to improve the quality of your life to direct electronic mandates to your cultural representatives that much more remote.

Naturally the bog-standard reaction to all such concerns is 'well if you don't like the system then leave'. Well, many people do yet those very same people that invite you to go blame you for the inevitable consequences of your leaving the politicians to carve up reality and dispense it back in paltry dollops and not helping them to resist that mindless drivel that always drips from the lips of demented democracies. The problem that arises is that when people do leave to find a better quality of life elsewhere large numbers of aliens need to be imported to fill the gaps that would naturally arise in a market that depends upon the price of homes being kept artificially high because if most people left, these worthless bits of tin and plasterboard would become valueless embarrassing reminders of the stupidity of ownership and greed.

Furthermore there wouldn't be enough idiots left to pay the politicians who unable to charge exorbitant rents for their cultural hovels would be forced to let them almost rent free so as to retain some satisfaction from having wasted vast quantities of the planet's resources on attempting to become modern day aristocrats, that breed of human that believes that the privileges that financial and military power permits are best served by keeping all the ill-gotten proceeds to oneself and any other tribal chiefs that might need to be bribed and paid off to keep quiet.

The nation to which you belong might be your ideal. Those reading this might say that their nation is the best and that people have no right to disagree and should be deported to some island and left to rot. Were that the case it would suit many to be deported and left alone to rot on some island in the middle of nowhere. The problem is that they wouldn't leave you alone because if your appeared to be getting along alright without them and actually began growing your own gear, brewing your own stuff and generally enjoying life this in itself would drive the one world theorists towards the edge and thus they would come with their ships and guns and their latest illegitimate moral and ethical pontifications that are always used by the intellectually subnormal to justify gross acts of interference in the affairs of others.

Such retards are totally incapable of grasping the fact that individual self-determination within and guided by a culture that can be freely chosen is and always will be a universal and absolute right of all living creatures. This culturally guided and guaranteed right for individual self-determination precludes the moral and ethical authority of political and religious synthesised intellectual constructs to outweigh and override those universal precepts that are hard wired into the intellect of humans in order that they know when they are acting outside the bounds of honour, decency, justice and fairness. It is only the culture of a nation that can clearly define where these boundaries lie just as it is only your chosen culture that is able to tell you when you come too close to the edge. But when nations go beyond their permitted boundaries and start to slide into that mindless oblivion that stupidity and greed invite all to be in, they attempt to drag down others with them, lashing out wildly in an attempt to come to terms with their own vulnerability and clinging unmercifully to the innocent and the disinterested so that they may not have to endure their self-inflicted culturally sterile hell holes in total isolation and without others to blame.

25 Whatever Happened To ... ?

WHY MUST OTHERS pay for the greed, the incompetence, stupidity and inefficiency of others as well as being forced to suffer through the bigoted violence that such intellectual defects make inevitable? Why must those remote from and unconnected with western economic industrial, commercial and political absurdities be forced to suffer the political, economic, social, cultural pollution and environmental degradation that such systems produce? Well, in the one world theory of those deranged democratic dictatorships this planet belongs to and was created by some deity who inexplicably decided that brute force and ignorance should be the method by which half-witted apes would transcend their spiritual and intellectual limitations and thus be fit to enter into the next stages of creation. The idea that they might be wrong could not enter their minds because their political and economic systems were founded upon a philosophy that not only despised cultural codes of civilising conduct but detested wisdom, prudence and fairness because these things would limit and confine such incompetent baboons to a one world and it's ours that nobody else would actually want. Thus, they saw immediately that their wants must be our wants, that their world must become our world.

Great nations therefore arose that seized upon the brutalising forces that science and technology could make available, not caring at what cost to others their vile potions and poisons were forcibly extracted from nature's strongholds. A perverted delight arose in the minds of such wretches when they were encouraged and permitted to spread their vapours and effluents to distant and remote areas of the globe and from such places, they imported large numbers of living creatures in order to mutilate and deform them in a futile and pointless and painful attempt to prolong their own wretched and miserable existences. But such wretches still believe that they can actually legitimately own and control other living beings because their own intellects have never been allowed to fully develop. Such people still believe in letting science blunder blindly forward in the hope of uncovering some great unifying truth which however cannot and does not exist in a material or numerical form. Their belief that one can isolate and refine, distil and evaporate, combine and divide, compress and heat, glue and stretch a single and vital link of that great chain that holds this world together without such a reckless and blinkered attempt leading to a world that starts to fall apart at the seams has led to a system of basing everything upon its immediate benefit to some at the long term expense to others.

But such a cultural absurdity is of no consequence because such people believe that if you accidentally stumble across something, or steal something, that you have invented something. The problem with inventing something is, like all inventions political, intellectual or religious, that they are completely useless and worthless unless others can be forced to want them, forced to need them and forced to buy or pay for them.

If we had need of them in the first instance, we would have been given them by our creator free of charge. As stated, the principle of sufficient reason states that an object possesses only that which an object needs to have in order to function properly and efficiently in the first place and all its subsequent needs are met freely and without conditions by its culture.

To ask for more or to take more is simply a form of greed. Inventions, physical or intellectual, therefore if superfluous to your requirements are totally unnecessary. But to a particularly nasty breed of human inadequate this idea sent them over the edge and thus they entered a world occupied exclusively by those demons and malignant spirits that plague the minds of those that possessing nothing in themselves that others would naturally want decided to create and synthesise and invent the concept of ownership, this simply meaning that they would go out and take what wasn't theirs and that did not and still does not belong to them, call it their own and then force others by and through a fear of that violence that one always associates with those close to the edge of reason and legitimacy to buy or pay for that of which they have no need or was theirs in the first place.

But as then as now and as will always be, whatever junk has been invented or manufactured, harmful or degrading or indestructible, must be forced upon others otherwise it is useless and worthless. An irrational fear of failure and a furious hatred and contempt for those that reject such so called unsolicited advances naturally arises in the hearts of those thus spurned and those malignant spirits and demons that fill the intellects of those scientific, military and political adventurers must be avenged and placated by a world-wide campaign of terror tactics to force others to accept their culturally worthless and insignificant tripe so that it doesn't lie around uselessly rotting away in some shed on some industrial estate in some dowdy and miserable cultural backwater in some seedy downtown area of some seedy nation.

Thus the collective creativity of mankind to produce great and civilising cultures has now been replaced by an obsessive fiddling around with just about anything, this excessive scientific and medical meddling thought essential in generating enough wealth to fund the conversion of the world into a single unified political and economic system based entirely upon possessions and ownership and if others ignore the wondrous political and financial pills and potions with those cure all ingredients that cut mankind off not only from each other but which also sever those roots that keep his feet firmly upon sound and stable ground then they will be forced to pay the price, like it or not.

When technology discovered the power of the electron to put iron and steel into motion and to guide it with great precision and realised that this simple electronic charge could be harnessed and stored, modulated and modified and fired from a magnetically guided gun to reproduce whatever reality they wished to present to others then it became possible to redefine those age old yet ill-defined concepts of value and worth, the two being synonymous in the minds of many.

The value of an object is a numerical interpretation of its worth. A sheep is always worth its own weight in meat and fleece and potatoes and apples always provide the same worth of nutrients, weight for weight, yet their value alters appreciably. Modern tin and plasterboard culturally sterile hovels are more or less worthless and meaningless in the quality of the life that they afford to their occupants yet their value in financial terms always grossly exceeds any reasonable or acceptable amount.

The reason for this has already been stated, that is, the invention of privacy and ownership and state sponsored political and religious terrorism, yet with the coming of the electron whole nations could be persuaded that this is how it was meant to be, this is how it must be and this is how it is going to be as long as others are in control of your planet, your earth, your home and your environment and your physical and intellectual destiny.

When whole nations begin to base their cultural concepts upon the electronic transposition of objects to another time and place, sitting room or wherever, they lose their original meaning and identity because like photographs they capture a moment that belongs elsewhere because that moment is a time related independent to the future glimpse into a past that cannot be of retrospective value to those viewing them in the future. No matter how hard one tries, you have moved on and the electronic past has become irrelevant to the future yet if a machine could be produced that makes the past the present and the present could be stored and converted into the future then people could be manipulated into living in the present, a sort of anything possible world, a timeless existence that could view the past, present and future at the touch of a button, locked into a limbo by their transfixion by those plasmatic editions of a two-dimensional, perspectively modified colour enhanced time unrelated reality that would cut them off not only from that true reality that needs to be dealt with but from themselves so that their 'self' never gets anywhere except to work and back onto the sofa to watch yet more of their valuable and irreplaceable time drift aimlessly and uselessly away.

Reality itself becomes a distraction, an uncontrollable and indefinable fear that lurks just off the edge of the screen, ever ready to spoil that willingness of the many to lose themselves and lose those precious seconds and minutes in an electronic fantasy world in which no pain is felt yet in which the flickering photographs of that which had just passed before the mind have been prearranged and ordered to leave the self emotionally drained without any physical or intellectual interaction being wanted or desired by those involved in these one way unidirectional interfacing with one's culture.

To avoid those annoying distractions, those nuisances that would disrupt an already distorted perspective upon life, such as children and partners inadvertently blocking the view, bigger and bigger picture propagators need to be sought so as to block out real reality and to exclusively watch a pre-digested, pre-formulated and prearranged digitised version that will proclaim the need for everyone not only to have a goggle box but the need for everyone to pay the price, either directly or indirectly of other people's need to become culturally isolated.

Once people become convinced that they are somehow inextricably and indelibly politically, religiously and electronically linked to others then a sort of self-righteous hypocritical indignation arises in their minds, encouraged and fostered by their jailers and keepers, that those that wish not to support the parasitic elite and their political pornocracies deserve less than nothing.

But the whole purpose of life is not to be politically, religiously or electronically linked to others if no cultural safeguards exist to ensure that such linkage is fair and just, that such interaction is balanced, that the individual counts just as much as the many and that the part is as great as the whole.

Television has become the ideal medium to define a modern world in which a two-way balanced interaction is not possible or desirable, for whilst the population of western nations remain emotionally traumatised by watching personal relationships being destroyed by people's inability to behave properly or decently the parasitic elite and their cronies are artificially and maliciously inflating the cost of houses and homes whilst debauched democracies are dreaming up new and offensively divisive rules and regulations to make themselves immortal.

In a world torn apart by political incompetence, religious bigotry combined with unrestrained scientific and medical meddling and a fetish for numbers, ownership and a desire to control all forms of life, the resultant world is an 'us' and 'them' socially fragmented structure which permits the state to blatantly own and control their miseducated slaves to consumerism whose value is only judged upon their numerical wealth and their inability to function as free and culturally independent entities.

This world of synthesised electronic and linguistic unrealities is upheld by and through the fear that its owners and controllers, already dangerously close to the edge of reason and legitimacy, might in a fit of hypocritical political outrage at some trivial irrelevant jibe at their deranged and derisory democracies might press the button or throw the switch and thus consummate an incestuous relationship between the state and its imperial guards by obliterating all forms of life in the belief that such a course of action is in accord with the wishes of some hypothetical and mystical super being who has chosen might over right and intellectual incompetence over cultural acumen.

All living creatures born into such a cultural wasteland must at an early age learn to swallow their pain for if not slaughtered or mutilated, caged and dissected or driven to extinction they become public property to be used and abused at the discretion of their mentally retarded prison guards.

The offspring of human kind are encouraged by the state not to be pampered with that time, love and affection that their parents need to give to them in order that they may slowly and steadily mature into those confident and independent and affectionate creatures that this world is in desperate need of and thus many are shoved into 'sure to start badly' state run indoctrination centres where they are hemmed in and monitored day and night whilst their parents struggle to afford their tin and plasterboard prison cells. If they fail to cope with the stresses and strains of these modern day uneconomic unrealities that result from the stupidity and greed of others then when little Jonny returns home after being traumatised by well-meaning indifference he is forced to watch his family being torn apart as they struggle to come to terms with themselves and a world that is in a constant state of change and flux in order to keep its paper promises in motion.

When the inevitable happens and people, lacking control over their own lives and their own environments, lose what little control they have left over their feelings and their emotions, they turn against each other in a sudden frenzy of fear.

As soon as the first signs of domestic division and strife appear the passive side of life batten down the hatches desperately hoping to become passive victims of their own foul-mouthed abuse of their partners whilst the active side of life vent their frustration in outlandish acts of physicality desperately attempting to control and resolve the situation using their rationality and power.

A whole unwholesome breed of state sponsored wretches then appear from the woodwork, a band of culturally insignificant mutants composed of well-meaning incompetents who mix in with their inefficient meddling a gender ridden hatred of those that are assumed guilty, these combined with the now obligatory law mongers in shiny suits that tout and trade amongst the bloated and rotting remains of a once loving and affectionate relationship.

But little Jonny has no choice but to suffer and little Jonny's parents have no choice either because those cultural safeguards that should be in place to remove those stresses and strains that lead to the premature failure of relationships have been deliberately removed and discarded to make way for the one world super state that has taken it upon itself to define reality according to its own warped and distorted visions of what constitutes justice and fairness.

Great, all-inclusive cultures, understand the needs of their members and thus they are designed to protect the individual from themselves as well as from others. Because your culture recognises you as being a unique and irreplaceable human being that has something of value and worth to give to yourself and others it upholds the concept of reciprocity, this concept denying the right of others to arrest or detain you upon unsubstantiated, flimsy, trivial, unsustainable or transient accusations or suspicions. Before any action can be permitted to occur those that make any accusation whatsoever must put their cultural credibility on the line and clearly state the reasons and upon what foundations such charges are levelled at a particular person or group. A cultural court would then decide how to proceed and if those that instigated such proceedings were found to have laid false charges then they would in themselves, be liable to a penalty equal to, if not greater, than that which would have been suffered by the accused. No matter who accuses who, those that make accusations must be prepared to accept the cultural consequences of so acting.

But in nations that possess no true culture and have thus invented a cartoon replica which inhabits a transient and fleeting electronically generated world whose ethereal mists of computerised unsubstantiated reality float before the eyes of the numerically mesmerised, in this world in which anything is possible everything that appears before the mind demands an immediate response because everyone is forced to live in the present because all of life is presented 24hours/day this electronically generated continuum requiring an instant reply. Thus, no matter what if an athlete has just finished a race they must reply to inane questions whilst gasping for breath or if a politician says 'red' another must immediately reply 'blue' and if a disaster occurs an immediate enquiry must be called for. Worse still in the 'it's possible world' of the rationally retarded nothing is allowed to rest because it is possible that the C.I.A. the KGB, M15, the pope, the man with the squeaky bicycle and the Martians did conspire to alter that truth and reality of an event and thus inquest after inquest, enquiry after enquiry must occur because even the demented dribblings of a bunch of intellectual cowards and incompetents can now catapult this world into a war because it is thought possible that a nation armed with antiquated and obsolete weaponry could destroy the combined nuclear arsenals of the west; but is it likely?

In nations that possess no real and worthwhile culture and thus its citizens can have no intrinsic honour or cultural credibility then one monkey can poke sticks at another or accuse another of doing the same without any fear of reproach, without any fear of retribution and without any concept of the correct and proper behaviour to be expected of and from them because nations without true and easily definable and accessible cultures that guarantee the quality of life that its members can expect and that prescribes how its members are to conduct themselves the few are totally free to spoil it for the many. Such nations are to be regarded as uncivilised ones that are best ignored.

However if such nations force their unwanted attentions upon others, either directly or indirectly, or force others to suffer the ill effects of their vile vapours and poisons as they struggle to come to terms with their own inability to understand what they are doing in their quest to generate vast quantities of those non-essential trivialities that have become so essential in keeping their worthless paper promises flying around at supersonic speed, then such nations can be regarded as environmental terrorists.

If a nation attempts to foist upon others their own diseased version of a political system that depends upon a numerical interpretation of reality that distorts logic and rationality by and through the assumed propriety of deciding moral and ethical issues upon the relative magnitude that one empty and meaningless set of numbers can achieve above and beyond an equally meaningless and unproven set of numbers because as numbers must refer to objects and those objects in themselves might be totally unfit to be counted. Nations that force others to adopt such systems should then be regarded as political terrorists.

If you are born into a nation that deny their men folk those absolute rights necessary for them to act as free culture creating individuals and that deny them those fundamental rights that belong to the active half of creation alone and to no others, then such a nation is guilty of sexual terrorism.

Cultural accountability is that by and through which all things will be finally judged. This reckoning up of what each individual has done with their creative powers is that which decides their future. To reckon means to explain and thus all human beings will be required to explain themselves in front of and before their creator who is bound to accept the collective decisions of those cultures that true men have created to decide their own fate.

It is of no consequence as to what created the intellect within man, for whether it be nature or whatever, for this final reckoning only decides who will progress to the next stages of existence.

To avoid that wilful self-imposed ignorance that so many employ to claim that they are innocent of any cultural crimes, intellectually valid and competent cultures explain mankind's responsibilities and duties, that is, they make them plain and intelligible even to the most intellectually incompetent. Such is the skill of creative cultures in making mankind's responsibilities to itself and nature evident to all that it is only those imbeciles verging on idiocy that need special guidance.

But in a world where the feeble-minded rule then anything becomes possible if those so afflicted have no culture, and thus have no codes of conduct or criteria of correctness by and through which to judge the imbecility of their actions.

Thus if the feeble minded combine their intellectually subnormal talents with a breed of social inadequates that resort to mindless violence to mask and hide their lack of social graces and this band of cultural misfits adopt an offensively discriminatory political system based upon an illogical numerical system of defining the value and worth of those moral and ethical definitions of reality that they force others to adopt then this world becomes something else other than what it was or could be or should be.

It is therefore the moral, that is, that which is enacted on a day to day basis to demonstrate one's cultural beliefs, and the ethical, that is, those concepts and ideals that define and decide how one will act upon a daily basis, duty of all human beings to either create a culture or to nurture a culture so that life can return to its original and intended meaning.

All journeys into the unknown have to start somewhere, it matters little where one begins the cultural jigsaw. Decadent culturally sterile nations delight in inflicting all forms of pollution upon the populace mainly because this form of environmental degradation so degrades the physical and mental abilities of those forced to suffer the effects of the indiscriminate use of chemicals, radiation, noise, misinformation and social and sexual terrorism that little or no resistance is possible to halt the advance of intellectually senile and offensively discriminatory control mechanisms to turn people into state owned and controlled dysfunctional robots that exist as landless and mindless peasants without any of those rights and privileges that are necessary for them to function as intended.

Pollution is anything in the wrong place at the wrong time. Water is essential for life but in the wrong place e.g. your lungs it is fatal. Chemicals are in themselves harmless unless in the wrong place at the wrong time. But decadent nations delight in pumping out filth because they believe the world belongs to them and thus the rest of mankind, being of no consequence, must pay the price.

In culturally advanced nations every type of potential pollutant would be monitored whether physical or mental, political or religious, electronic or chemical, sexual or social, financial or cultural. Culturally advanced nations understand that those mental and intellectual pollutants so favoured by western deranged democracies and their feeble-minded dictators are just as dangerous as physical pollutants.

Accordingly, culturally advanced nations assign all of their members with a cultural credibility rating which explains to others the degree of cultural competence that the individual has reached in an understanding of how they relate to themselves and other members of their culture, their environment and those that have adopted different lifestyles.

The cultural credibility of the individual is thus available to all. Furthermore, the cultural credibility of everyone in public office is made available and every item made or produced would be encoded so that everyone could look up the cultural credibility of the nation, the people or the company that produced it. For example, if a chemical company produced potential poisons and failed to tag them and follow their progress to ensure safe use and disposal then such a company could be held accountable and forced to explain their actions.

Great cultures therefore exist to make people accountable to others and to explain their actions. A lot of religified drivel is talked about final judgements and forgiveness but it is up to the culture of a nation to make these final judgements, and it is up to the culture of a nation to decide if it is possible to give away their absolute right to condemn and thus exile those who refuse to act in an honourable and upright manner.

It is up to the culture of a nation to guard and protect its members by removing and exiling those that lose their cultural credibility and thus make them unfit to live amongst those that wish to live in peace and quiet and in harmony with their environment. People possess an absolute cultural right to live unmolested by the intellectual and social inadequacies of others and so competent cultures enact prescriptive laws that predefine the quality of life that must be upheld throughout the nation. These laws therefore ensure that all houses and homes are fit for their intended purpose and that those that live in them create a neighbourhood with a guaranteed quality of life that precludes those with little or no cultural credibility, no matter how numerically rich, from entering into and spoiling the environment of others.

In decadent culturally sterile nations any 'tom, dick or harry', if numerically rich can buy up great tracks of land, fill it with shot gun fodder, hire mindless wretches to slaughter all other forms of life in order that such gun toting financially superior scum can fly in once a year to exact a vicious onslaught against defenceless creatures. Yet such people are the darlings of decadent democracies because they symbolise the very essence of the 'us' and 'them' society upon which all democracies depend.

It is of no consequence that a silent and sterile landscape appears devoid of its natural occupants because in culturally backward nations money is allowed to talk and thus becomes the international language, not only of the usurer and the profiteer, but of the politicians and their state hirelings.

In great and civilised culturally competent nations it is cultural concepts that do the talking and money is forced to be quiet because it is bound by cultural codes of conduct and gagged by everyone being granted the essentials of life in recognition of their absolute right to exist as independent well-informed individuals that have been created for a unique and special purpose.

It is only your culture that can freely provide that information necessary for you to avoid inadvertently aiding and abetting those who wish to control this planet through and by a numerical supremacy and failing that, like all greedy and financially spoilt brats, will attempt to destroy that which they cannot possess or control.

It is only your culture that can protect your cultural identity and allow you to function unmolested by those that would steal it and use it to abuse or falsely or maliciously accuse you because in the intellectually incompetent world of the feeble minded mud only sticks because those that throw it are protected from any form of accountability because such worlds have never even heard of cultural reciprocity and even if they had they would refuse to try and understand its implications.

Thus it is only your culture that can provide you with that pollution free sanctuary which is yours by right, which is yours alone and in which you can turn around and sort yourself out and you are guaranteed that time and space, that cannot be invaded by others, that is necessary for you to come to terms with yourself, your existence and your culture.

It is only your culture that can possess the moral, ethical and intellectual authority to give you your cultural credibility just as it is the duty of your culture to ban and to exile those cancerous and malignant influences that wilfully and deliberately destroy the lives and the environments of others.

It is only your culture that can truly represent the individual and the totality of those truths that they have chosen and thus it is only your culture that can reach those universally binding decisions that alone can earn the respect of any creator.

It is only your culture that can uphold the dignity of man by ensuring that he is guarded against all those schemes of spite that are hatched by those jealous of his active and creative role within existence.

It is only your culture that can uphold the absolute right of true and free men to exercise complete control over their own environment and to ban those who, being unable to control even their own emotional and intellectual instability, have no right to steal from him that which is his alone.

It is only your culture that can issue you with your true identity and thus it is only your culture that will and can protect your cultural copyright that no one can take from you and use without your permission.

To steal is to take without permission, thus a thief takes without consent. In the cartoon cardboard cut-out culture of degraded democratic numerical dictatorships all citizens, being regarded as publicly owned state controlled entities cannot object to having their photographs taken nor their genetic codes, nor their thumbprints, nor their blood, nor their children, nor their goods or homes seized upon the flimsiest of reasons because in a world in which anything is possible then all becomes not only acceptable but also probable.

Great cultures therefore prescribe and define consent and thus it is only your culture that has the moral and ethical authority to create those cultural contracts that predetermine when permission is needed and when it is not. This predefining of the moral and ethical environment for its members enables competent cultures to avoid those tediously mindless trivialities that infest decadent nations when one monkey insults another and the whole troop scratch and shriek and jibber on and on desperately trying to screech louder than another in the forlorn and futile hope that something constructive and sensible will mysteriously arise from the latest offering from the chimps' tea party.

In political systems that are above and beyond any cultural control and that are justified exclusively upon totalitarian principles in which the numerical consequences of pretending to allow a permissive electorate to decide the degree of moral and ethical depravity that they are willing to accept from the culture of their nation then those that tout for votes amongst the wreckage of decency, honour and truth are forced to behave like consumptive itinerant tinkers whose inbuilt inability to consummate their promises before the next bunch of meddling and incompetent wasters are shoehorned into the life of the nation leads to those that find that they cannot deliver what was not theirs to give in the first place into adopting a defensive approach which having no legitimate causation leads onwards to those that assume control to frittering away their somewhat limited mental capacities upon an obsessive attempt to demolish and then reconstruct that universally rational intellectual framework that defines the true, proper and fitting role for mankind in his journey through this existence. They do this in the forlorn hope that this reconstruction of their own peculiar version of reality will somehow justify their own superfluous and inessential roles within the proper functioning of life itself.

Realising that they are in effect illegitimate manifestations of the power that greed and stupidity have over the minds of the superstitious when the fear of pain is combined with a fear of eternal damnation they resort to a sort of numerical mumbo-jumbo whereby one set of meaningless in themselves symbols are shaken and stirred and cast upon charts and graphs to indicate if the omens are good or bad or to decide who shall live and who shall die. The magic of numbers not to implicate those that resort to them in any dubious or dishonourable behaviour or intentions leads to a belief that numbers in themselves possess a latent and mystical power that is released when they are counted and thus when enumerated they have the ability to reach a total so totally disconnected from reality that those who come to rely on them are in effect immune from the consequences of living by numbers.

A whole new counting culture thus arises in which everything has to be, to be real, to be counted and thus have a number. Accordingly, all moral and ethical issues become numerical ones and thus the degree of depravity of an individual is not contained in what was done but how many times. A killer who murders a dozen is far more deplorable than one who kills just one or two unless they are the 'enemy' and so the reverse is true, the more of them that are killed the better. High court judges must judge life according to a numerical frame of reference. If some deformed specimen of humanity can be cut up and reformed into a passable rendition of reality, no matter how sterile, no matter how painful the process, no matter how distressing both to themselves and their guardians then no matter, as long as the matter so formed can exist numerically longer than it would otherwise have done then that's alright and everything is hunky-dory.

But everything isn't alright, and everything cannot be, for numbers are simply part of an inflexible pre-set, self-regulating, non-unitary, abstract system of assigning hypothetical relative values to those objects to which they refer. To believe that any living object should be subjected to such a system that in itself is totally incapable of predetermining the quality of life is an absurdity that is difficult to account for. If living beings needed numbers to determine their value and worth, then we wouldn't need to be taught how to count. But individual living organisms are simply not related to or dependent upon or made by or are naturally subservient to numbers for they are dependent almost entirely upon the quality of that life created by the culture of their parents for them to be born into. It is the culture of their parents and thus of their nation that predetermines how that creature develops. It is only the legitimate culture of a nation that can transcend the physical and intellectual limitations of those rigid political and religious systems that to have any justification at all are entirely dependent upon a numerical interpretation of value and worth. A political party with half a dozen members or a religion with five members, no matter how fanatical is of no greater or less significance than those of unlimited numbers for intelligence is limited whereas stupidity isn't. Great all-inclusive intellectually coherent cultures are those flexible and creative entities that employ the creative talents of true men to establish and predetermine the quality of life to which all its members have an equal share. All such members have an equal responsibility for ensuring that the cultural world created runs smoothly and efficiently and that all living creatures within that world advance together in a unified and cohesive manner, none being seen or sensed to be taking advantage of another.

If the world that you inhabit is in a mess then you can either create or join a culture that will cure it or blame it on others and do nothing or adopt a westernised approach and fiddle with the figures and tamper with reality and stick your headphones on and buy a goggle box so big you cannot see past it – either that or become politically aware and spend your time attempting to damage and mutate those fundamental principles of honour, justice and fairness and turn them into those numerically sequenced digitally enhanced lies and falsehoods that the western hemisphere uses as its cultural criteria to judge the degree of its own moral and ethical depravity as it employs vast quantities of electronic gadgetry to recreate this world into a 'one world all pals together' existence which excludes everyone and everything that detests and thus resists the globalisation of those democratic dictatorships and those chronically destructive commercial enterprises upon which they depend. The invention for a need for the needless is what drives such uneconomic economies and destructive democracies and inevitably leads, like all inventions, to a belief that this world actually belongs to those who think that they invented it.

But such is the hold that numbers have upon the minds of those that are forced to count everything before they can walk or talk properly that they come to believe that such symbols when combined with a fetish for staring at objects through lumps of glass and seeing things that were not visible before are improving the quality of their lives because they actually believe that they are learning something and thus progressing.

Thus, if an individual has learned something and is progressing, which is doubtful, then they come to believe that they must be clever. But to prove to themselves that they are clever requires numerical proof, a quantitative analysis of how worthy this cleverness is. Thus, the really clever, to be really clever, must award themselves and their cronies as many lumps of glass and bricks and lumps of plasterboard and as many numbers of financial units as possible. However not everybody can be allowed to be as clever as they are because everybody would start awarding themselves whatever they wanted. Thus, everyone must be controlled by force and made too long to belong to that exclusive group and be forced to go along with what the clever tell them is true. The clever are thus charged with using their ingenuity to trick people into believing that numbers are essential and that electronic gadgetry is essential and that paper promises are essential whilst keeping and hoarding unto themselves those true essentials of life and putting them beyond the reach of those that truly need them.

The only possible means that the majority of people in such nations come to believe that they could ever 'really' really belong is to become numerically rich and thus whole nations become spellbound by tawdry and culturally demeaning tombolas in which the fate of the many is decided by the fate of a few numbers that promise yet another culturally pointless and meaningless day in the lives of both winners and losers. This is because numbers can only buy numbers. Nothing has actually changed apart from the fact that the world has become a more divisive and a sadder place, a breeding ground for extremism, a more pathetic planet on the edge of some forgotten galaxy drifting towards that universal oblivion that awaits all who claim that they are innocent of creating by collusion, either actively or passively, those cultural poisons and intellectual and environmental pollutants thought indispensable in keeping the inmates of the state run asylums in a drug induced cloud cuckoo land in which every impossibility is promised yet nothing actually arrives. Whether love is the drug, or food or junk it matters little, overindulgence obliterates the pain and sorrow of living in that never land wherein nothing worthwhile ever lands on your doorstep. You have no choice but to live the way you do because the one world theory states that there is only one way, one political, economic and religious system, a one-way street to salvation. Whereas in reality it is just an endless road to nowhere with nobody to greet you along the way.

It is only all inclusive and cohesive cultures that can offer their members any real choice of which road that they should take to achieve spiritual satisfaction. Such cultures assist their members to be mentally, physically and economically and emotionally free by ensuring that they are born into and grow up, develop and mature in a world that is the 'should be' world that we all know could exist and not the 'what is' world that all seem to accept as though it is a numerical inevitability.

In the totalitarian state owned asylums of the west what 'should be' cannot in fact exist because such a world would represent a legitimate and worthwhile expression of man's inalienable right to self-determination using his intellect rather that his calculator.

This skilful non-numerical interpretation of an idea or an emotion would create many possible worlds, many possible choices yet all contained in one prescriptive definition of reality. These new worlds could not be measured, fixed, owned, bought or sold or classified because they would be mobile, flexible, creative worlds yet remain true, coherent, accessible and intellectually coherent to all mankind.

It is only your culture that can skilfully combine the many ways that mankind expresses its natural joy of life and of living into one united symbol of mankind's natural desire to live in peace with itself and its environment. It is the job of the western money grabbers and political degenerates to destroy the quality of life and turn it into a joyless and miserable daily grind and to shove as much trivia and tripe down the throats of their landless peasants as possible.

To such people if a world cannot be bought with promises or subverted with threats of violence then it must be destroyed by weaponry, chemicals and electronic poisons or any other illegitimate or degraded means.

This is because if individuals were to grant themselves any real and worthwhile choice between a cultural world based upon truth, justice, honour and fairness and one based upon a jealous greed that defines worth and value numerically then if the number of cultural converts threatened to significantly deplete the coffers of the parasitic usurer and those political and religious deviants that they employ to guard and harass their drones and slaves then this 'other world', having only reason and honour to defend itself, would be destroyed using that indiscriminate and mindless violence that one associates with the intellectually challenged as they stumble around attempting to justify the unjustifiable by appealing to the power of numbers to numb the conscience of so called civilised nations.

It is only your culture that can prescribe with an axiomatic certainty what you will and can expect for it is only your culture that can enable you to discover who and what you really are in yourself because the mirror that it holds up to you reflects what exists within your very soul. It portrays you as you are and it portrays you as you could be. No secrecy or distorted lenses are required to build up false hopes and great expectations for what you see is what you get, that is, those mental and physical freedoms that permit you to advance and progress in a proper and straightforward manner.

Your culture gives you the time and space not only to develop correctly but gives you that security that comes with that constancy of purpose that does not and will not change and thus individuals are permitted to slowly mature into well-formed intellectually competent and complete entities that in themselves are those distinct and recognisable spiritual beings that alone can demand and receive that respect that belongs only to those who have the cultural credibility to be thus honoured.

But in a world dominated by stupidity and greed and a fetish for numbers, property and ownership great cultures cannot arise because great chunks of this planet and that reality that belongs to them are simply stolen and reprocessed and stored away in huge secret vaults deep within those capitalistic nations that fritter away their miserable existences counting one culturally meaningless number after another.

If such nations were to allow people to choose which cultural criteria to adopt in order that they may live by those precepts that they believe will make their existences meaningful and worthwhile, whilst preserving the balance between humans and their environment, so much the better. Furthermore if such nations were to allow people to choose a stable and consistent environment unruffled and unaffected by those ridiculous manifestations of political and religious incompetence and degrading and often illegitimate flights of fancy that puts the needs of their groupies and hangers on far above that to which justice and equality dictate then two worlds could exist – one that is stable and consistent in which people's expectations are not cruelly disappointed when a new bunch of mentally challenged half-wits are elected into positions that require skills and abilities far beyond their comprehension and an ever changing unstable world dominated by that jealous greed and mindless violence and a fetish for interfering with others and their environment – all driven by an acute awareness of the moral and ethical illegality of using and abusing people and their environment and their absolute right to a fair share of this planet's resources – all this combined with that intellectual incompetence that would, if removed, demonstrate to them their total lack of cultural awareness.

But elitist one world supremos treat everyone who do not bow down to them as anarchistic reactionaries because they do not understand that there is a middle ground to which nearly all life belongs in and upon but the very existence of which has been denied and the possibility of its re-emergence strongly resisted by the use of economic, political, religious and social terrorism.

But terror breeds fear which breeds violence which in turn breeds fear and that fear brings instability and a perpetual and never ending quest for that peace and tranquillity that only and can only exist in that politically and religiously excluded middle ground in which no person or object is permitted to transcend its own physical and spiritual limitations and rise above others in order to gain those marks of distinction that turn them into those peculiar specimens that believe that others will be dumb enough to go along with this absurdity. Yet whole nations are struck dumb by that fear that is deliberately instilled into people when their children can be snatched from them, their homes taken from them, their environments stolen from them and abused and misused, when their so called neighbours can award themselves obscenely disproportionate benefits for controlling their lives and when the nation to renege upon their promises which it never intended to keep declare themselves bankrupt ensuring that the usurers and profiteers are well prepared beforehand so as to convert their ill-gotten gains into gold, silver and lumps of mud.

If a new breed of intellectual reactionary anarchist emerges to remonstrate with such people they would simply be ignored because the elite live in a world controlled by force and the fear of force, this force being feared because it is an indiscriminately irrationally applied pressure to make everyone conform to the latest hypothetical absurdities pronounced by the latest set of intellectual incompetents to be put in charge of running the state owned and controlled social asylum. But the pressure applied is a discriminatory one for true pressure acts with equal force in all directions, that is what equality means. But to the elitist riff-raff and scum it means downwards only – to put down and suppress any legitimate claims to an equal share of this planet and its resources and the natural right to live as a free and self-determining individual unfettered by the parasitic exorbitances of the ruling elite.

When one is forced to remain as a dumb spectator whilst the seas are mercilessly dredged dry and all its life forms slaughtered to extinction, and when one is forced to accept that great forests have to be laid bare so that the west can grow fat upon the cattle that graze there and then to be told that the only way that you can change this world to a better place is to trudge along to your local church hall to vote into power yet another set of party propagandists ever keen to prostitute their honour and to destroy their consciences for a few lumps of mud and bricks then this intellectual absurdity puts most people in the west on a par with those root crops in their vegetable baskets.

But being a basket case with the intellectual integrity of a potato is now what it's all about because you would never have to slave for the system again and you could push to the front of the queue in your supercharged electrified basket chair. Obviously that bunch of political incompetents that promise you the most get your vote every time because in a world that lives by numbers it is what you get that matters and not what you could get because in a world where promises and agreements last only as long as it takes for the ink to dry it is a grab it while you can cartoon land where time is condensed into that fractionalised zone between one synthesised picture of reality and another before the state flicks between one of its promised pictures of political, medical and economic perfections to the next.

But a sense of loss and a deep feeling of spiritual isolation remains embedded in the hearts of those that trudge this lonely road to cultural oblivion. This universally felt feeling that there ought to be more, more to life, more for the self and more for others cannot be assuaged no matter how many boxes of goodies Santa brings. The lonely life of the plasticated child formed and moulded out of a need to conform by its plaster-of-Paris parents, set hard against each other and against life itself forces whole nations into an apathetic acceptance of the inevitable consequences of living a lie, the first and greatest of all sins, to lie to oneself, to lie for one's nation, to lie for a few more numbers and thus to eventually lie outside the purpose of life itself and thus to lie beyond the reach of humanity and ultimately beyond the reach of its creator.

This feeling of cultural and intellectual inadequacy forces whole nations to continually seek reassurance from other nations and like all cultural delinquents whose lack of moral sense and social competency are caused by having an unstable, unbalanced, unaffectionate and a financially uncontrolled upbringing causing them to be emotionally and spiritually insecure, they hang around waiting for the approbation of like-minded cultural inadequates whilst lurking behind secret schemes of vindictive spite to pester and interfere with those other people who regard them with that contempt which they deserve. Immediately the unstable delinquent senses disapproval or indifference to their demented drivel about how powerful and important they are they draw up a vast list of sanctions against those people that refuse to sanction their authority to make any universally acceptable or legitimate proclamations concerning reality.

This constant seeking for attention by those culturally incompetent nations who are infested with self-interested intellectually retarded apes who squander vast sums of numbers to banish those physical reminders that they are in fact trapped inside the body of a monkey, this need for an identity beyond the obvious drives their 'anything is possible' cartoon cultures to become more real than reality itself, which to them is slow and boring because they end up being forced to live in and with themselves, and thus time and space must not only be altered and modified but other people's time and space must also be changed and thus the whole quest of western nations has been to steal that time and space that belongs to others. A timetable must therefore be drawn up that others must follow, or they will feel the full force of the west's military might. Space itself must be filled with that electronic gadgetry that keeps an eye on other people's living space. The technologically advanced nations must not only control the time and space of others, but they must make this new reality available

24/7 upon goggle boxes so big and powerful that those that watch them cannot see beyond them. Everything must be made instantly available so that the past and future are the present.

Unfortunately for the 'one world and it belongs to us' intellectual and emotional inadequates the past and the future are not so easily controlled. Nevertheless the past can just be made into a whole series of interconnected historically inaccurate events mixed with statistical and numerical lies delivered out of context and dubbed over with a one sided perspective, the whole synthesised heap of tendentious tripe being made entirely relative to the retrospective over exaggerations of whoever could claim to have over indulged their fanatical need to exact an inhuman and disproportionate retribution against those that may have displayed a self-interested greed that outshone that of the eventual victors, this medley of sanitised selective memories being hauled out every time someone begins to question the validity of the here and now.

To the one world theorists if everything can be put in the present tense and everything that has, is or will happen can be made instantly and always available at the push of a button then truth and reality will become entirely dependent upon who controls what is said or done now and not upon what was said or done or what will be said or done.

Accordingly, the true past does not and cannot belong to you and thus you have no true and honestly available cultural heritage.

Equally you cannot have a true and honest future because the future cannot exist because of the constant need to change and synthesise reality now.

Thus all those pieces of paper that promise a proper and decent and honourable future for you and your family cannot do so because even if you were foolish enough to believe in paper promises of a better world just around the corner if you eat up and swallow the pitiful and painful world today such promises have to, like all promises be based upon a stable and consistent environment, both social and political, that cannot in fact exist without strong and creative cultural controls over those jealous self-seeking political and religious bigots that infest all life forms with their parasitic schemes of antagonistic envy and spite.

The cartoon replacement cultures of the west to be what they are, that is fast moving renditions of a synthesised reality, must be in a constant state of flux, a never-ending process of one inconsistency after another. Just as reality is about to re-emerge and spoil the view the walls turn to custard and the sea evaporates into a mushroom whilst a super hero is resurrected out of a broken umbrella and manages to zap everyone with their triple ionic delta ray gun hyper spaced in from alpha centagron, a planet in the fifty fifth dimension on which Elvis has been living for the past two centuries.

But to those brought up in an anything possible world that boggles the brain with numbers and the phantasmagorical effects of watching an electronic box in which a cartoon culture is available all day everyday has upon it then anything, no matter how ridiculous, improbable or absurd can be presented ipso facto before the mind and the mind has no choice but to accept it, not only because it has been shown to exist by the fact that it appeared on a lump of glass that is your supposed cultural gateway to truth and reality but because there is sod all you can do about it anyway.

It is of no consequence whether you believe what you are shown or told because if you disagree they'll come and bash you up and take away your children if you have any and your furniture if you have any and they'll give your partner or your neighbours or themselves everything and they'll steal your cultural copyright and they'll enforce the state's right to own you and your soul because after all you're just a landless peasant who doesn't deserve to exist at all.

Accordingly as you are in reality no more than a state owned and controlled living organism stuck firmly in the present tense with no past and no future and without any absolute rights or choices and living without the protection of any culture that would enable you to become independent to those that wish you harm then if this is so you must be a slave to the system and a prisoner that whilst it is fed must entertain itself at its own expense by clinging to those synthesised versions of reality that attempt to gloss over those fleeting images of a world being destroyed and mutilated by stupidity and greed and that imports vast quantities of trivial tripe in an attempt to hide the vast quantities of rotting carcases that have been created by the needless slaughter of those creatures thought necessary to uphold your westernised democratic values.

It is only your culture that can create a true and workable future for you, one that is more than a set of numbers upon a piece of paper or card with a few balloons and ribbons thrown in. If you make a contract with your culture then that is it – it will be honoured, independent to time or space or numbers or political or religious comings and goings. If you say 'I do' it is done, now and for always, not 'til this or that changes because this and that in constant and intellectually valid cultures cannot and will not change. If you say 'I will' then you must or you will become a cultural outlaw banished to that bedlam reserved for those cultural cowards, usurers and political parasites and deviants that look always to themselves and not to others. If you say 'please' it will be a pleasure to serve you. If you say 'help' you will be helped not by numbers, not by promises of help, not next week, but at once – for your culture is your only true and reliable friend that exists because you exist and without you it is less than it could or should be. The fact that you in yourself are an integral and essential part of the culture to which you belong gives that culture its meaning and purpose and thus its authority. Your culture thus cannot and will not lie to you because you, being an indispensable part of it, will immediately know that you are being cheated. Your culture makes no promises that it cannot keep for the promises that your culture makes are ones based upon love and affection, of support and interest and these things are free to give and free to receive because they belong in the very heart of your soul, they are what your soul is essentially composed of, a disinterested affection for all living creatures and a yearning to be one again in one great universal chain that alone can recreate the true meaning and purpose of life.

That feeling of separation and isolation that arises when one simply exists without any cultural safeguards cannot be described or success-fully conveyed to others because the gap across which they must travel has become filled with that trivial junk upon which the economies of the west have come to rely.

Your culture will not make you numerically rich, it cannot make you financially successful, it can only provide you with the basics of life, freedom from stress and isolation and give you a deep sense of belonging.

It can show you what it is to be immortal for it shows the soul which route to take to become an integral and invaluable part of this and all future existences.

Your creator cannot, in fact they refuse to help you because you have already been given all that you need and to demand more is simply a stupid and demeaning form of greed.

Your politicians cannot help you because they are too busy helping themselves.

Your neighbour cannot help you because they will not possess those truly transferable cultural values necessary because in the west all cultures, native or imported are of that peculiarly tribalistic type that sets and keeps man apart from man. It is only you that can help yourself and thus others. It is therefore the duty of all true men to create a culture that transcends the religious and political bigotry and dogmatism that is responsible for turning this planet into a one sided world funded upon the globalisation of stupidity and intellectual incompetence combined with a fetish for interfering with other living creatures and all driven by an insane desire to achieve that immortality that alone belongs to those that employ their intellects to establish a living environment in which honour, justice and fairness reign supreme and in which mankind can transcend their own individual physical and spiritual weakness and thus become those complete and integrated easily recognisable and welcomed entities that alone are worthy to exist throughout that time and space that has been created for all those who prove themselves worthy to inherit them.

This one and only everlasting true reality awaits everyman that is prepared to be not only true to themselves and true to their families and true to other families and nations but is also prepared to be true to that culture which they are responsible for creating and protecting. Their culture is in return responsible for prescribing what everyman must be prepared to be in themselves in order that they may be true to themselves, true to their families, true to other families and nations and true to their creator and ultimately for deciding those who are worthy to continue their journey through existence and those who are only fit for eternal oblivion.

It is therefore only your culture that in itself can be a true democracy because all, each and every vote counts because all and every action taken by humans upon this planet will not only be taken into account and thus have to be accounted for but the decisions taken by all members of a culture as to whose actions are to be condemned and whose are to be applauded are binding because they bind our creator to honour the choice made by his creations for it cannot be otherwise.

In The End

THIS INTRODUCTION TO culture and masculism demonstrates the need for true men to exercise their rightful authority to create a universally benevolent culture that denies the right of the state to act as the final arbiter.

It is the culture of a nation alone that is responsible for deciding how we behave, and it is the culture that one is born into that decides who is fit to live on after death and who are only fit for eternal oblivion.

Your culture is your one and only true and constant friend that alone has the power to transform you into a universally beneficial entity that is welcomed in all possible existences.

But being in this world today is like being in some huge factory full of machines and electronic gadgetry with workers whizzing around ignoring you with nobody prepared to tell you why you are there or what your job is or how you actually got there or were sent there in the first place.

Worse still, nobody asks your permission to do what they do, they just do it anyway no matter how badly the smoke, steam and sparks may affect you, you are given no choice but to either stand and gawp or be told to stand at a machine all day and pull the lever when the light flashes. You have no choices, you have to accept that this is how it is, and this is how it's got to be.

But if you have courage you will demand to know, demand an answer that makes sense. You will demand that the workers stop and listen and if they refuse then at least demand that they show you where the exit is but even this may be denied to you.

However, if you belong to a strong cohesive and easily identifiable and accessible culture then it is only this union between sense, honour and decency that can show you the way out just as it is only your culture that can show you the way into your 'self'.

When one finally becomes oneself by becoming an integral part of your culture then that culture can then confer upon you those honours and distinctions that transform you from a transient unattached entity into a spiritual force that can not only demand recognition as being worthy to exist now and in any possible future existence but that must and will receive that recognition.

The following verses are dedicated to those who are so busy selling themselves for a few lumps of mud and tin that they never have the time to discover who or what they are.

Their fellow travellers through time would return and try to rescue them but they cannot because those who waste their time attempting to become part of a reality synthesised out of the stupidity, greed and incompetence of others become unrecognisable entities, one of those lost souls that inhabit a world of perpetual oblivion in which having only themselves to blame spend all of eternity blaming themselves.

The outstanding ability of humans to not only destroy the past with their lies and distortions of reality and the present with the stupidity of greed and a fetish for numbers but by denying their proper role within creation they come dangerously close to destroying their future both upon this planet and in all and any future possible existence. Their whole quest appears to be to spoil things for others if they cannot have it for themselves thus modern man fearing nothing beyond what numbers and science tells him is real arrives at nothing having blundered around wildly in his attempt to become a transient somebody and ending up as a perpetual nobody.

The End

In the end there's nothing.
You arrive and it's just a void.
Space – empty space.
There's nothing there – just an empty space.
You journey and keep on going 'cos you believe, or just don't know.
It all goes away.
You arrive expecting all sorts of wonderful things.
But there's nothing: like a house where there's supposed to
be a party but it's empty and dark and dull and slightly damp.
 – empty – just a blank wall with fading memories.
What's the point? Well, there isn't one: just a long series
of fooling yourself into believing that when you arrive
they'll all be waiting for you with lots of presents and
food and laughter and good times and happiness and keep right on to
the end.
But in the end, there's nothing.
Just a hole where heaven should be – or was.
It's gone – stolen, taken, lost.
What was isn't anymore.
Don't fool yourself – don't strive.
You get there and you realise that there's nowhere else to go.
You've finished and there's nothing more to do, nothing more
to see, nothing more to feel.
The world withdraws and ebbs away.
You stand alone and look around but there's just nothing.
The material world dissolves into a tissue of fading thoughts.
You stop thinking – too dull to feel.
You ache with the sick empty realisation that it's just
a pointless journey into a grey boring nothingness.
You stand and rot in silence in an eternal misery that cannot end.
You cannot die, there's nothing to kill yourself with –
you just have your faults, your pain, your flaking scabs,

your inadequacies.
You stand in your own filth and rot in space –
a space that has no defined beginning or end –
just a rot hole in the fabric of so-called life
held together by the tissue of lies told to you
when you had faith – but all that is left to you
is a dull aching for what might have been.
You open the box and it's gone – just empty space occupies
the place of your hopes and dreams, the mirror on the lid
mocking the grotesque image of imperfection and uselessness
that you have become.
Your mask flakes away leaving the red raw reality that
you are a not wanted, not loved, not liked, not cared for,
not missed, a not wanted surplus to requirements
piece of existence that stands slowly rotting away in some forgotten hole
in the void.
And when you arrive at the total finality of
your empty existence you discover that nobody or no
thing will ever pass by you or see you or think of you.
You become so isolated by your physical and mental deformities
that even if you could return to end your misery you have
become so far removed from that false reality called life
that you would become a phantom in that nightmare called
loneliness.
You would become that fear, that terror that all wish to
avoid yet all arrive at with the same silly expectations.
But no matter what was expected, whatever it was has gone.
Destroyed or stolen or just never was.
You become a fixed permanent nobody filling the whole of
your universe with misery and pain – a self-perpetuating
horror that would pollute and contaminate any creature who
accidentally fell into your pit of misery.
But no creature ever calls or falls into your pit and
throughout time countless pits are formed into which
drop those who come after you in the hope of finding
what is now gone.

Postscript (2022)

As the Western World descends even deeper into megalomania, it becomes clear that their diseased, dictatorial democracies are forced yet again to pollute and contaminate truth and reality.

It is said that supreme power is controlled by being vested in the citizens of those nations that have chosen such a peculiar system to rule their lives.

However, what security can other nations expect if those citizens belong to the same class as their rulers, who appear to live in a fantasy world that ignores crimes past and present, and who, when called to account for their uncivilized conduct and behaviour, simply 'spit their dummies out' and begin screaming and screeching at full volume – hoping to drown out the beliefs and opinions of others, as well as attempting to divert suspicion from themselves for what has happened and what is happening.

One may well conclude that the shock of another nation standing up against the West and its sick and weedy cartoon culture reveals that the Western nations are no more than a united bunch of war-mongering, brainless, disease-ridden baboons, who will stop at nothing to try to prove how supreme and infallible their worthless democracies are.

The Universally Valid, Logical, and Rational Order of those Cultural Controls necessary to manage the Conduct and Behaviour of Human Beings

Cultural Contracts and Laws
Culturally enforceable Codes of Conduct and Behaviour
Culturally Educated Creative Citizens
A Culturally Controlled Civil Service to ensure Justice and Equanimity
Religious and Spiritual Societies
Political Movements and their Governors

It has now become self-evident that when political movements deny their subordinate role within civilized societies, they quickly become uncontrollable and unaccountable entities.

When this happens, it becomes the ethical and moral duty of all sensible and rational citizens to issue a Proclamation that denies their leaders and their leaders' allies and supporters the lawful right and authority to act against those supreme obligations given to all individual entities by their creator to nurture and protect those who are defenceless against those indiscriminate acts that terrorize their fellow inhabitants, because they possess the weapons but not the justification to act in such a manner.

Proclamations

A Proclamation, which means a 'Cry from the Soul of Humankind', is a God-given Right and Duty.

The term 'God' means 'that which created existence' and that entity who designed and encoded our DNA in order that a living being could arise whose brain had the power to create not only consciousness but also a conscience.

It is your conscience that decides not only whether or not you uphold the honour and dignity of created existence, but which forms also that essential part of the mind that has the power and responsibility for engraving upon your Soul what steps you have to take to protect those fellow beings that are powerless to protect themselves.

Specimen Proclamation

I, William, a citizen of this Planet, declare upon my Honour according to that Universal Authority granted by my Creator, do hereby reject and disassociate myself from the actions of those political and religious movements that use indiscriminate acts of senseless violence against defenceless human beings without restraint, without mercy, without common sense, and without any logical or rational justification.

To remain silent when others act upon those dangerous beliefs that are generated when whole nations combine their subjective, synthesized relative beliefs of religion with the contingent relative numerical truths of their corrupted political ideologies is not only a cultural crime, but those whose voices remain silent, and whose pens remain idle, can only expect to become one of those lost souls who being ostracized upon this planet will be destined for eternal oblivion in any future existence.

William.

Naturally, you can give yourself a personal identification number, so that if you wish to send a copy to a website so as to form a universally valid petition, your Proclamation has a first (or any) name, plus your style of writing, plus a PIN, and so will forever remain a unique testament that you stood up to be counted, which, after all, is the reason you were created in the first place, and once you have spoken, that's all that really matters in the end!

Plebiscites

Plebiscites become necessary when governing bodies elected to govern according to the wishes of their electorates fail in their duty to put the interests of the common man before all else, and by doing so attempt to usurp their mandated authority. If such an event happens, then those laws and reforms enacted by that governing body become illegitimate acts, for they act against the mental and physical well-being of the citizens of that nation, who have given their governors the right and duty to act in an honourable, dignified, and humanitarian manner.

When usurped authority acts against the common good of a nation, it becomes the absolute duty of the common man to proclaim a Plebiscite that demands those constitutional reforms necessary to avoid democracies degenerating into dictatorships that ignore the fact that their legitimacy and authority are based entirely upon that supreme power belonging to the common man alone.

This self-evident truth is upheld by the fact that when dangers to the sovereignty and independence of the nation arise, it is the common man who rises up to defend those beliefs and freedoms necessary to ensure that a stable, universally valid, civilized and humane culture is protected against those evils associated with those that cheat and lie to feather their own nests.

For a Plebiscite to be rationally and logically valid, all those eligible to vote must declare upon their honour that they have read, fully understood, and wholly assimilated what this decree means.

This declaration that they have the mental capacity to fully understand, as well as grasping the consequences of their own actions, gives such a Plebiscite full sovereignty to reform those machinations of the state that act against the common good and well-being of its citizens.

Equanimity

It is the culture of your nation that is entirely responsible for ensuring that you are guaranteed 'peace of mind', that is, your culture promises to enforce its 'Codes of Conduct and Behaviour' in order that you can live in peace and harmony with your family, your neighbours, your environment, and most importantly, within yourself.

To achieve this, your culture balances those base animal instincts of Pride, ignorance, Greed, and Stupidity against those human virtues of Humility, Understanding, Generosity, and Sense. However, as stated, great Civilizations and their universally valid cultures require True Men to protect them against decadent and diseased dictatorial 'demonocracies'[1], for without True Men, cultures shrivel and die, and when cultures shrivel and die, then so does the truth and so does our creator.

---

1   The word 'demonocracy' is the original meaning of what the ancient Greeks decided to call a 'democracy', which was designed to elevate the top twenty percent of the pop-ulation that were entitled and encouraged to control the remaining 80 percent by lies and brute force. Thus, the West gleefully adopted a political system that was designed to become the ultimate political trap: the 'catch numero uno' – you can only get rid of us if we ever let you – which we won't. The elite can therefore only be eradicated by dem-ocratic means, but as they have absolute control over the meaning of language and thus the meaning of words, then no matter what is said or done, they remain an irre-movable political absurdity, just like the idiots that thought democracy was a good idea in the first place.

Since most Western nations have no universally valid, all embracing cultures to educate them and ensure that the Mind of Man is taught those intellectual and logical absolutes necessary for his reason to become rational, logical, powerful, and sensible to the needs of others and their environments, then we require a Reformation to put the monks back into their monasteries, in order that they may spend their time healing the sick, giving the land back its health and nutrients, offering sanctuary to the lonely and distressed, and writing down in their great manuscripts those wise, rational, logical, and eternal precepts necessary to illuminate the four corners of this planet, as well as the four parts of the brain, to show how to have a sensible conversation with each other.

To set the mind at rest requires it to understand what the Real and True purpose of thinking is.

You do not have to think about running your bodily functions – your hormones and proteins and most of your brain are in charge of that!

However, your frontal lobe, which is responsible for higher-level thinking, requires not only good nutrition, but good tuition. It is entirely dependent upon getting a good – meaning well-balanced – instruction manual to tell it how to think clearly and correctly, which makes 'the self' what 'the self' is – both in itself and in its 'body and soul.'

The mind, therefore, needs a good 'workshop manual; that tells it how to look after itself, as well as what it needs to do when it's not running well at all.

Of course, in great civilizations and their universally valid cultures these workshop manuals and their contents are freely available, and those intellectual precepts necessary for the mind to think clearly and have the capacity to be taught how to think (and NOT what to think) give the mind peace and tranquillity.

Those precious precepts that are safeguarded by your culture instruct the mind of the order in which it must put the information it receives before it is examined by its ratiocinative, inborn powers of thought. These ratiocinative powers – meaning to think formally and logically, that is, by observing the rules that govern logical thinking – enable the intellect to avoid confusion and muddled thinking.

Beside me as I write is an article from the *Guardian* newspaper (an opinion piece by George Monbiot) asking 'Why is Britain's mental health so incredibly poor?' – in other words, 'why are we so miserable and confused'?

Well, ask your prison guards, your money-junkies, and the religious freaks, as well as those that teach only what your demented 'demonocracies' tell them is needed to keep the political parasites in power. It will necessitate a Cultural Reformation to put culture back where it belongs – in charge! Not only will it recharge your soul, your family, your mental health, and your cultural rights and duties – it is your only true friend, since it allows everyone to participate in the running of the nation.

Common sense prevails!

The appendix gives a short list of those major precepts that need to be understood and the order in which they are best studied.

Good luck!

The Beauty of Simplicity

In cultural terms, Truth means the Beauty of Simplicity.

Beauty means 'A self-evident, well-balanced, visually pleasing, self-generated mental image of an objective reality', while Simplicity means 'easily understandable and easily put into the mind without fear of being confused or misled.'

Throughout history, it has been recognized that human beings are composed of distinct parts, namely Body and Soul. Whilst it is recognized that the material part is short-lived and easily damaged, the spiritual part has the capacity to become immortal, if it is correctly protected and nurtured, educated and loved by an all-embracing, universally rational and logically valid set of rules and regulations, which form those laws, contracts, duties, and codes of conduct and behaviour that time has clearly demonstrated need to be honoured to avoid the loneliness, isolation, distress, and misery that those who live for themselves are bound to suffer from.

Yet, whole nations have arisen that destroy those cultural safeguards necessary for their citizens to enjoy stress-free lives, and who instead are left completely controlled by a scientific, industrial, medical, and numerical interpretation of reality.

When this happens, those True Men who are responsible for protecting those everlasting truths that are the only true source of legitimacy, honour, dignity, and justice are bullied, threatened, terrorized, or imprisoned so that the state may control them using peculiar, diseased, and illogical self-relative, self-generated subjective beliefs to ensure that those cultural safeguards of justice and equanimity shrivel and die.

But when cultures shrivel and die, then so too do civilizations; and when civilizations die, then so does the truth; and when the truths dies, then so does our creator; and when our creator dies, then we return to those wild, irrational, war-mongering, brainless apes that put themselves and their tribe above and beyond all else.

When truth and simplicity die, whole nations are forced into accepting the inevitable consequences of living in a world of deceit and lies, and must then create the technology and means to invent and uphold the deadliest of all spiritual evils: to lie to oneself, to lie for one's nation, to lie for a few more numbers, and to lie down and refuse to help those who are daily slaughtered, all to uphold those dictatorial demonocracies that exist outside the purpose of life itself, and thus lie beyond the reach of humanity and so beyond the reach of ever being forgiven for their inhuman crimes

Appendix

To ensure peace and equanimity requires the mind to be given the right intellectual tools and a 'cultural workshop manual' that explains 'How to think simply, clearly, and precisely, and correctly', and thus avoids those that 'Teach you what to Think', and who uphold control, and own the numbers and languages that they must teach you as being the only things that you need to make sense of reality.

In this Appendix is a very brief guide to the intellectual tools necessary for the intellect to distinguish truths from falsehoods, and how best to assemble such truths in their correct order of importance, before they are presented to the mind. Thus created first is an idea, then a concept, then a belief, and then finally a true and logically verifiable conclusion.

A brief guide on how best to use the inbuilt ratiocinative power of the human mind to understand and simplify complex propositions.

Pure logic tells us that all that exists inhabits a four-dimensional world, the truths and realities of which are easily accessible if the mind is given the right tools and instructions.

Whatever is presented to the mind for its intellect to examine needs to be given its correct truth value before it can be further assessed using the four dimensions of pure logic that it already possesses to determine the rationality of that which comes before it.

When the mind blankly accepts what it is shown and what it hears without firstly determining its truth value and its correct truth classification, it is wide open to believe all sorts of nonsense, which if left unchallenged results in confusion when it is presented with conflicting evidence.

Before all else, the conscious mind needs to be advised by its conscience to ask itself to test all incoming information with the use of four basic questions, so that received information can be classified according to the Four Truths of Reality it belongs to.

The intellect therefore examines the information and asks itself, 'Is this an example of an Absolute Truth, a Relative Truth, a Synthetic Truth, or a Contingent Truth?

If the ratiocinative powers of the intellect decide that it is an Absolute Truth – a self-evident, categorematic, stand-alone absolute that is a word or words or imagery or a set of symbols that represent an irrefutable reality which transcends all attempts to stop it standing alone – then it can immediately be accepted into the mind without further ado.

If a statement or proposition claims to be an Absolute Truth, then the mind must ask itself: 'Is what this message claims to be true related to a particular or peculiar event? Is it a self-evident proposition? Who or what claims it to be an obvious, well-established fact?'

If what is claimed appears to be related to current events and seems to be a particular truth to a particular people or particular nation, then it is a Relative Truth – a truth that cannot be universalized and is therefore stored away as having a subordinate place and role within discussions concerning those true realities that it claims to be apposite to.

Synthetic Truths are those which are self-justifying and relative to a particular mental set of abstractions that possess no material or tangible form, such as mathematics, man-made laws, religions, political ideologies, and other intellectual abstractions not essential to a healthy and worthwhile existence.

As they are unable to be universalized, because human beings are now incapable of creating a universal rational, logical, just, and equitable set of rules and enforceable codes of conduct, then humans are now forced to exist in a limbo of fear and trepidation that their leaders, who are already close to the edge, might spit out their dummies and press the button.

Contingent Truths are based on contingencies, which are completely dependent upon unrelated events that come together to create an event that cannot be foreseen as their meaning is usually purely coincidental.

Contingent Truths are therefore retrospective truths that are relevant to different times and different sets of circumstances.

Consequently, Contingent Truths cannot be brought into the present tense unless one wishes to create mental instability by introducing such truths into a Universe of Discourse that is considering issues of current importance.

Universe of Discourse, or Frame of Reference

Pure logic requires the mind to deal with one Truth at a time.

It therefore encases and protects that Truth by choosing a safe place for it to remain while it is being examined, thought about, and discussed by those languages of the mind.

The languages or language of the mind needs to create a 'holding pen' for the material it is analysing, thus no other information is allowed to enter this 'refuge for clear thinking, and as Plotinus states, 'Once you have uttered 'the Good', add no further thought by any addition, because in proportion to that addition you introduce a deficiency.'

Accordingly, Agonic Logic uses a four-dimensional geometric object of Pure Ratio that can exist in material and abstract forms, and in both conditions it is an Absolute Truth that cannot be altered or denied, and that can protect what is True in itself ('The Good') from idle minds, self-relative truths, and those logically illegitimate, synthesized human abstractions such as numbers, their demonocracies, and their laws.

Agonic Logic therefore uses a square into which one proposition is placed at a time. This square becomes the 'Frame of Reference for the Universe of Discourse' – that is what you are talking about or abut (pronounced 'aboot' or 'wot yer talkin' aboot' in Geordie).

This comes from hill-billy land: the sheep are gathered from the fells and put into various pens while some are left outside, and so all the sheep are either 'in a pen' or outside it – they cannot be 'sitting on the fence' or they would fall 'outside' or 'inside'. The ancient word 'abuta' is very important for logical thinking, because it denies the old logical idea of 'or', since it is logically self-evident to the 'mind's eye' where a particular sheep truly is.

However, as all sheep tend to look the same, they each receive their own PIM (Particular Identification Marking) so that no disagreement or logical disputations can arise in the mind – that is, you do not have to argue with yourself whether or not to believe the evidence of your own eyes.

Once inside its pen the idea created by that information delivered to the intellect is marked as representing either an Absolute Truth or Reality, or a Synthetic Truth, or a Relative Truth, or a Contingent Truth.

The mind can now deal with the 'imprisoned' proposition by simply making the four sides (dimensions) of the Frame of Reference – the square – either an Absolute, Relative, Synthetic, or Contingent reality: yes, you already have a good idea of what Truth value to give it (that is what logic is all about), but you can go further by asking, was the mind 'induced' into believing that it could be true, or has the mind deduced that it *is* true.

The difference between Induction and Deduction is simple to understand. Imagine you are on the Underground sitting in a carriage adjacent to another one. One starts to move, and you think that it is you in motion – that is, you are led to believe something by an outside event, yet when you look the other way, you will see that the platform and station are fixed and non-moving. You therefore lead yourself to the correct answer, and are not led or fooled into thinking that something is true.

Your culture represents that fixed, non-moving platform and station that is essential for keeping you on the right track!

The story so far:

We have   The four Truths of Reality
            Four-dimensional logic
            A Universe of Discourse
            A fixed Frame of Reference
            An understanding of Induction and Deduction, and
            We have turned an idea into a concept

We now need to release the imprisoned concept from its square and put it into a larger one to test it and see if it's fit to become a useful, specific but not universal belief – because beliefs are subjective realities and not universal ones.

In its new upmarket square with all mod-cons, the concept can now be analysed further to judge its value as a possible objective rather than subjective reality – that is, can it transcend from an Intellectual Abstraction and become a material entity – that is, can its four walls and itself be made into a tangible reality both in its structure and in its meaning – that is, the meaning of those words used to form the proposition that is being examined – that is, demonstrating in an objective, concrete manner what its material form means.

Thus, in civilized nations with a Universally Valid Categorematic Culture, which is in complete control of its politicians, its commercial enterprises, its infrastructure, and its security services, artisans are employed to create meaningful and easily understood representations of those immortal precepts that give the culture of a nation its moral or ethical legitimacy to act to keep its people free from stress, ignorance, and fear, and free to have an equal share of the nation's common wealth and to participate directly in local, regional, and national affairs.

The culture of your nation is directly responsible for ensuring that its children are well-fed, well-housed, and well-educated, so that they can think for themselves and thus directly participate in ensuring that their fellow citizens conduct and behave themselves in a polite, friendly, civilized, and courteous manner.

Once intellectually conceptualized abstractions become tangible realities by them being skilful representations of those concepts, they then reach the stage of being those believable entities that can be used to ground one's conduct and behaviour with some degree of certainty.

Before a belief can become Universalized and become a Categorematic Absolute it needs to be turned into an object of universal apperception, meaning 'the assimilation of a new sense-experience to those ideas, concepts, and beliefs already present in the mind of the observer, reader, or listener.'

Once a general or specific belief is broadcast by its being generally available in a tactile form such as a book that can touch the soul of mankind, then beliefs can and do become Absolute and Immortal Truths.

Your culture is the protector and guardian of those immortal truths that combine to form those universally valid precepts that when elucidated become the only source of that legitimacy needed before an individual, a tribe, a nation, or the world itself can act to create and uphold those realities that lie at the very heart of existing as a humane, fair, just, honourable, and dignified human being.

It is only a Universally Valid Culture that can create legitimate laws because the word 'Law' means 'How things lie in Reality'. The citizens of a nation are duty-bound to protect that common-sense reality and those universally valid, immortal precepts that the higher intellectual function of a healthy, well-educated intellect can clearly demonstrate are those categorematic absolutes created when a healthy brain decides to think in the four dimensions of reality. The true realities have been built and hard-wired into the brain so that the self can fully understand what the self needs to do to uphold that honour and dignity that is associated with being a being given the chance to become an integral and essential part of the eternal life of created existence.

Conclusion

WHEN EDUCATED HEALTHY brains unite, they then possess the universal right and obligation to employ their collective intelligence to create those culturally based proclamations that alone have the moral and ethical authority and justification to compose and write down a codex of those enforceable rules and regulations that nature and time nave proved to be absolutely necessary for controlling base human instincts.

These codes of conduct and behaviour are enshrined in a single entity known as a Universal Cultural Absolute, to which all nations are subordinate, and that alone has the legitimate right to control those nations that refuse to control themselves.

Universally valid cultural laws transcend all those synthesized abstractions created and employed by humans in a futile attempt to control those that seek to destroy the lives and the environments of those other nations that lie beyond and outside of their control.

When human kind realise that it is only by adopting a universally valid culture built upon those precepts made up of those everlasting truths that are independent of material existence, and which have been encoded into our DNA and made readily available to those humans that take the time and trouble to educate their minds so that their intellects can fully understand what their conscience is telling them, then human kind can knock on the door of truth and reality and be handed the key that opens the gate to eternity itself.

defassa@hotmail.co.uk

Appendix II

My FORTHCOMING BOOK will be upon the logic, truth, reality, and ratiocinative powers inbuilt to the human mind, and is written to judge what is self-evidently true and obvious and from this common sense to allow the mind to reject those faulty and illogical beliefs that lie outside reasonableness and thus beyond its control.

When certain poorly constructed, illogical, synthetic and hypothetical abstractions, such as numbers and languages, which can be controlled and deformed and made meaningless by other beings, are then forced into the minds of humans, then human life becomes a meaningless journey on the long road to eternal oblivion.

When the natural intelligence of a healthy, well-fed brain becomes completely controlled by a meaningless language that cannot be altered, changed, modified, or rejected, and is then threatened by a numerical interpretation of what is right or wrong, or what is good or bad, then numbers are allowed to be used to bully the brain into submitting to gross acts of inhumanity.

When human thought is forced to use a corrupted language, the validity and meaning of which is upheld by that fear in the mind of losing what little it can control, then human kind can no longer be considered humane.

To be a humane human being means to be a civilised, kind, tender, merciful, refined, polite, honourable, just, fair, dignified, understanding, and generous entity that puts the common good of all that exists before the individual self – for it is upon this humble understanding that the eternal life of a generous and humble soul depends.

www.ingramcontent.com/pod-product-compliance
Lightning Source LLC
Chambersburg PA
CBHW060848280326
41934CB00007B/966